*

MISFIT 2

MISTER
JOHN

MISFIT₂

MISTER
JOHN

STORIES FROM A LIFE UNEXPECTED

First Edition
ISBN: 979-8-9900202-2-1

Cover Graphic © John Curran
Cover Design by John Curran
Author photograph © Sue L. Harrington

Author website: misterjohn.me

Fonts:
Adobe Garamond Pro by Robert Slimbach
Bobby Donut by Wahyu Eka Prasetya

YAK Publishing
Publisher website: yakpublishing.com

DEDICATION

*

TO SINGLE PARENTS
THERE FOR THEIR CHILDREN
EVEN WHEN THEY'RE NOT

*

TO THOSE WHO CHOOSE
TO BE A PARENT
TO A CHILD NOT THEIR OWN

*

TO GRANDPARENTS
LIKE PARENTS
ONLY BETTER

*

TABLE OF CONTENTS

PREFACE

JOHNNY CAN'T READ

"What does it say?"

"I don't know. I'll just have to wing it."

That's what I want to do as I get older, wing it, because what I can't make out is almost always what I need to know, the important stuff. Instead, I too often take risks with things like instructions and warning labels because Johnny can't read… the fine print. Print so small that I need a magnifying glass. Meanwhile, the brand name is large enough to read from across the room, confirming what really matters in corporate culture. At least I'll be able to tell the doctor what product sent me to the emergency room, even if I might not know why it did.

Not as important, but no less aggravating, I also have a hard time reading books, printed on paper, with a smaller font size. To reduce the number of pages in a book and, therefore, the cost to print it, some publishers make the words smaller than legible. The opposite tack of those in Mrs. Winkler's sixth grade English class who wrote in flowery script on wide-lined notebook paper to meet her "just a page" criteria, which is why she later added the 300-word minimum to her writing assignments.

To make matters worse, some publishers even go so far as to reduce the number of paragraphs in a printed book because those blank spaces in between add up, creating more pages. I eventually gave up on the last such book I was reading with its page-long paragraphs. Reading the book was like listening to a telemarketer natter on while I wonder if they'll take a breath before I curse their existence and then hang up.

But mostly, I don't like the fine print because my inability to read the tiny type reminds me I'm getting to be older people. While my mind is still happily skipping down Sesame Street, my body is gradually breaking down on the downhill road to the marble orchard. The first warning sign came around my 40th birthday when I realized I could no longer get out of a chair without making noise. Noises.

It's not just my creaky joints either because as eyes age, they also lose their flexibility, reducing their acuity. Imagine that. Even eyes get stiff with age. Something I'm reminded of every time I watch a sporting event from the States and the National Anthem plays... "O say, can you see..."

"Not like I used to."

"You have glasses, you know!" (Sue adds to my stories whenever she can.)

Yes, I do, but I seldom wear them because they only help me see things far away, and things far away usually don't need to be in perfect focus unless I'm taking a photo, and the autofocus on my Nikon helps with that. I have trouble with those things just beyond my nose, my eyes working best with objects as far away as my drafting table used to be and my computer screen now is. Go figure.

That's why I'm looking forward to something I've never had - a large-screen TV with a high-definition picture... when I watch ice hockey. Because now, sitting more than a couple-two-three feet away from my computer screen, it's hard to follow the pixelated puck when I'm streaming a game. To make up for what I can't always see, I do what any "Yah, hey" hockey fan would tell me, "Watch the players, not the puck, and you'll know where the puck is."

Yes, but sometimes, I like to see it...

While it doesn't help me watch hockey, I have a visual aid - a magnifying glass my Grandma Curran gave me when my age was still a single digit. Grandma gifted it after I started collecting coins, started when she began handing down her collection once she was convinced I wasn't going to use a Liberty silver dollar to buy candy or anything else - still true, even after all these years. Grandmas know.

The magnifying glass that once helped me read the fine print on coins now helps me read the fine print, period. It's nearly as old as I am, but its "vision" is still perfect. Over the years, the magnifying glass has moved with me because it's one of my earliest memories of Grandma, and I knew it would again come in handy. Now it sits on my desk, within easy reach, thankfully large enough I can see it without its help... for now.

I told you all that to tell you this... because of my less than 20/20 vision, next thing you know, my hair will start turning gray... "Ahem..." (Sue, again...), I do my best to make sure I, and you, can read, without a magnifying glass, any book published with my pen name on the cover. That's why this font isn't money-saving small, why there are two spaces at the end of every sentence, and why paragraphs are short, to make reading easy on my, and maybe your, stiff eyes. I know it'll be easy because I've already read this book... it now your turn...

BETTER TOGETHER

The ski slope was so... cool. Built inside Dubai's newly opened Emirates Mall, it had to be, lest the artificial snow melt. Even before the mall featured penguins, yes, penguins, frolicking in the freshly manufactured snow, Sue and I were eager to see the ski slope, but not to go gliding (tumbling) down it - been there, done that - Sue, growing up in Alberta, and me in Wisconsin, where neither of us were keen on the sport.

Nevertheless, the "wintery" scene seen through an observation window on the mall concourse filled Sue and me with delight as we watched the many undoubtedly experiencing snow, artificial as it was, for the first time. We decided playing in the snow was one of those universal things, as even the adults acted like children because no matter their age or if they glided or tumbled to the bottom, the common denominator was sheer joy. The same joy I felt in my younger days whenever it snowed... until Ma told me to shovel the driveway just after the snowplow passed.

Snow was not unheard of in the United Arab Emirates, as there was the occasional snowstorm in the Al Hajar (Rocky) Mountains of Ras al Khaimah. Topping out at over 6,000 feet, rare precipitation combined with elevation made for snow, the real kind, even if only an inch or two, and didn't last long. The fluffy white stuff was still a novelty as the mountains were inaccessible to most, and most UAE residents were from locations that rarely saw snow, except at elevation, such as the Middle East, North Africa, and the Indian Subcontinent.

Despite the expected oddity of the indoor ski slope, built atop a shopping mall in the desert, just a few feet above sea level, the unexpected discovery of a second-floor bookstore in Emirates Mall put even bigger smiles on our faces. In the UAE, even more difficult than finding snow, the real kind, was finding a bookstore with English-language titles and then at reasonable prices.

What we found could've passed for a chain bookstore in the States or Canada. In addition to books, there were magazines, newspapers, CDs, DVDs, toys, posters, puzzles, games, and such. There was even a Starbucks, in case we missed the one on the mall's ground floor and another across from the bookstore's entrance. Yes, we could sit in the bookstore's Starbucks and people-watch patrons at the Starbucks across the mall concourse… but we didn't.

The bookstore was a welcome slice of Western civilization, found in shopping malls anyway, as long as we didn't look too close. Although it appeared Western, the two Starbucks helping with that, the Ministry of Information and Culture, a branch of the Emirati government, reviewed all printed material, anything deemed inappropriate for political, cultural, religious, or any reason, banned, or censored, often courtesy of a ministry worker with a big black magic marker.

"How was work today, dear?"

"Busy… I'm dizzy… from all the marker fumes."

While the government of the conservative Muslim country forbid nudity, in public anyway, even "excessive" displays of skin were blackened. Women's fashion magazines received lots of additional ink, with cleavage a frequent focus. Uh-huh. However, my favorite ever edit was a cover model's itsy-bitsy bikini bottom transformed into a pair of not-so-short shorts. Spotted in an Abu Dhabi bookstore, I regret not buying that magazine for the artful censoring.

Despite the lack of affordable English-language titles in the UAE, I didn't do without, as most of the books I owned before moving to the UAE moved too. Thanks to the first tip I received from an expat, Tom, who hired me, I saved a hefty amount shipping them via the United States Postal Service using an M-Bag. Two, in my case.

Old mailbags were what they were, picked up from the local post office. Stuffed with as many books as would fit, I then brought the bags back to the post office for weighing. The USPS charged around a dollar per pound, far cheaper than transporting them via airfreight or excess baggage. Cheaper because the bags took the slow boat to the UAE, their arrival not measured in days or even weeks, but months. Three, in my case.

Fearing books shipped in canvas bags would get jostled and/or rained on and therefore damaged, my solution for both problems was to stack similar-sized books into small piles and then protect them with plastic wrap. My books would stay closed and dry. Moreover, because the plastic wrap was clear, inspectors could check what the books were without unwrapping them. I adopted this technique for any books bought during my yearly return to the States, then transported back in my luggage.

So the surprise discovery of a UAE bookstore with affordable English language titles we'd only have to transport home, not halfway around the world, had Sue and I scouring the store, although often in different aisles. After a couple-two-three hours of browsing, Sue and I bought $400 worth of books, enough that the walk out to the car park provided us with an arm-burning workout.

In the twelve years I'd lived in the UAE before we found the bookstore in Emirates Mall, the only locally sourced book added to my collection was a gift from an Egyptian friend, Ghada, a computer programmer at UAE University. That book was an English-language copy of the Holy Quran, one I still have. One that came in handy years later after a couple of Jehovah's Witnesses came knocking at Ma's door in Waupaca, my (respectfully) waving the Quran in their general direction enough to send them scurrying like vampires at the sight of a crucifix.

Despite our memorable find at Emirates Mall, I couldn't confidently name even one title I purchased that day. I still have the books. I'm just not sure which ones they are. What I do remember is the lone CD we bought. There was the requisite background music as we wandered around the store, except this music was good. One song got our attention enough that the two of us, not hip to the latest tunes, asked one of the friendly sales staff - less than half our age - what was playing on the store's sound system.

"This song?... "Better Together" by Jack Johnson."

After buying hundreds of 10-dirham ($2.70) pirated Thomsun Original cassette tapes when I lived in Al Ain, Jack Johnson's *In Between Dreams* CD was the only non-pirated music I ever bought in the UAE. Even more difficult than finding snow or affordable

English-language books was finding legitimate music until the UAE finally cracked down on counterfeits to gain entry into the World Trade Organization.

With Emirates Mall located on what, for us, was the far side of Dubai and traffic what it was on a Friday (Sunday) afternoon or any afternoon, during the drive back to Sharjah, Sue and I listened to the CD... twice. A second song, "Banana Pancakes," was also a favorite, even more so after we purchased our property in Ecuador the following year.

Out to check out Dubai's latest and greatest mall, the one with an indoor ski slope, little did we know that before we returned home Jack Johnson's "Better Together" would become our song. Heard not in a restaurant, bar, or club but in a bookstore. It seemed only fitting, Sue, a librarian, and me, dating a librarian, that and it's always better when we're together... eating banana pancakes.

038

COMPUTERS? I SWEAR!

My computer homework, assigned by a human (I assume) professor, was to write programs for basic accounting problems using FORTRAN (FORmula and TRANslation), version IV, a 1966 upgrade of the programming language conceived in the early 1950s.

Stay with me now. The story gets better...

While it was homework, I couldn't do it at home, not in 1981, as there was no computer in the apartment I shared with stepbrother Jay, his wife Jean, and their two-year-old daughter Jayme. Nowadays, with Alexa and/or Siri making themselves at home, in your home, listening to your every word, recording your every action, telling you what to think, even when you're asleep, sometimes it's difficult to remember when computers weren't... everywhere.

Instead, I had only one option to access a computer, the University of Florida's only computer lab, located on an upper floor in an older building, one apparently without air conditioning... that worked. After checking in at the front desk, as reservations were required, I took my place at the assigned terminal and typed the code I'd written by hand beforehand using paper and pencil.

When satisfied I'd done that with no typos - computers fussy when it comes to typos - I'd run the program, hoping I'd gotten it right the first time. If I hadn't, I'd make alterations and then rerun it. Every time I got it wrong, in my head, I'd hear the same thing I heard at nearly every football practice - Coach Mike Shanahan screaming, "ON THE LINE! RUN IT AGAIN!"

Grading on an extreme curve, only two grades were possible for the homework - 100% and 0% - either the program worked or didn't. If that weren't enough pressure, I would only have an hour to get it right or wait another four days to get back on a terminal and try again. That was all the time I could get with demand far outstripping supply - only one lab for 27,000 students… Those were the days, my friend.

I earned a B+ in the class, missing an A only because the only day I was absent, of course, I missed learning the formula for calculating how many loops a DO LOOP would run, and it cost me on the final, a paper exam. Still, earning an A in every other class, the university awarded me an out-of-state tuition waiver. That second semester, my tuition, paying the in-state rate, was only $270. I think it costs more now… Those were the days, my friend.

My first experience with a computer was a distant one as I sat at a terminal connected to a mainframe somewhere on campus, maybe off. At least I had a terminal with a screen and a keyboard to access that mainframe because at my next stop, the University of Wisconsin-Platteville, their only computer lab, had no terminals. There were keyboards, though… attached to card punch machines.

If a tingle didn't just shiver down your spine, once upon a time, computers read holes, not words, punched in cards, translating the location of those holes into the language the computer understood. Matching the size of the old "horse blanket" U.S. dollar bills, those cards, made of stiff stock paper, dated to the late 18th century, used to "program" looms and other cloth-making machinery. A hundred years later, Herman Hollerith paired them with his tabulating machines, a core product for a company-to-be called IBM.

In the lab, with demand again far outstripping supply, my first wait was for one of those card punch machines. Like almost every line I've ever waited in, mine was the slowest - a crumpled card, a jammed punch, some guy who'd have to improve his typing to match a chicken's, or just some eejit... I felt so bad for one guy and was so desperate to get going that I typed his cards for him to an appreciative round of applause from those in line behind me.

To be fair, there was immense pressure on the typist because if they made a mistake, they'd have to pull the card, insert another, and try again, there no Backspace key or white-out remedy equivalents for a hole punched in error. With even simple programs requiring a couple-two-three dozen cards, mistakes were inevitable, especially with a line of impatient and often agitated people looking over the typist's shoulder. Add to that the cacophony of all those students stuffed in an undersized and overheated lab with card punch machines clacking away, it was difficult to concentrate on such exacting work. Even the piles of winter clothes were not enough to deaden the noise.

You probably want me to explain that... OK... At the heart of Platteville's campus was not a quad, a football stadium, or even a library. It was a cemetery, a daily reminder that your student loan officer would follow you to your grave. Already a chilly walk past the tombstones on the wind-swept campus, it was even colder in winter, so I wore sweatpants, a heavy coat, a stocking cap, and insulated gloves, clothing I immediately removed once inside the lab because it, too, lacked air conditioning... that worked. The scene was bizarre, with students scurrying about, dressed in shorts and t-shirts, their winter wear piled everywhere like the mudroom in a typical rural Wisconsin home come the cold and snow.

Once I'd punched my cards, I held the stack with a "Kung-Fu grip," because if I dropped the cards, putting them back the way they were was... not fun, computers fussy about the order of things, like punch cards. While I was careful, the odd other was not, dropping their card stack, they then getting the same applause as a restaurant busser with a pile of shattered dishes lying at their feet. Why I was (eventually) always packing... a rubber band.

The next wait was for the card reader, this line moving faster though as there was nothing more to do than feed the beast by placing my card stack in the machine. Then I'd walk away, fearing my cards contained a typo. A fear I'd dwell on for 45 minutes, time for the computer to process my cards, spit out a printout, and for some lab assistant, shuffling behind a wall of pigeon holes, to put out my output, calling out my name as they did.

I'd grab the printout as if it were my lottery ticket, the winning numbers just called, to see if I'd won...

"ON THE LINE! RUN IT AGAIN!"

By then, I'd already invested over an hour in the process, only to find there was a typo. The computer, as computers do, wouldn't say what my error was...

"I know something I won't tell! I won't tell! I know something I won't tell...

Because how else you gonna learn, dumbass!"

Scanning my output with the critical eye I thought I'd employed the first time around, I'd locate a typo. Then I'd again stand in line for a card punch machine, retype the card, replacing the bad with the good. The process tested my patience with another trip to the card reader, followed by another 45-minute wait…

"ON THE LINE! RUN IT AGAIN!"

There was a second typo. Such frustration made for a long night in the noisy and sweltering computer lab, my ears buzzing, sweat dripping from my nose…

"Will the reader reject a card with a sweat stain?"

"No, but a soggy spot might jam it up."

Finally, finally I'd get output, typo-free output, only to find my coding was in error.

"I know something I won't tell!"

"Fuck you!"

"ON THE LINE! RUN IT AGAIN!"

"Shut up, Mike!"

Of course, any changes meant a return to the card punch and card reader queues, then another 45-minute wait for output. Inefficient as the process was, I didn't see much future for computers. How NASA sent astronauts to the moon with even more primitive computers was mind-boggling, even more so that they brought them home safely.

While I had to wait 45 minutes for output, at least I didn't have to leave the lab to get it because at my next stop, the University of Wisconsin-Milwaukee, students had to go to another building to get output from the mainframe accessed by a terminal in the School of Architecture and Urban Planning's computer lab.

Nevertheless, that lab was where I saw my first color computer screen. I would've seen my first color printer there, too, but the School of Architecture and

Urban Planning administration kept the $30,000 contraption under lock and key, forbidding anyone from using it, afraid it would break. So, while the school had a color printer, in reality, it didn't. Instead, to get color "output," students set up a tripod-mounted camera, threw a black cloth over the monitor to eliminate glare, took a photo of the screen, and then got the film developed… Those were the days, my friend.

Owing to my time in those three labs, I swore several times and one time swore "NEVER AGAIN!" would I use a computer. However, my tune changed in my second year of graduate school after I, with no other option, enrolled in a computer-aided design (CAD) course. One of twelve guinea pigs in the architecture school's first CAD studio, I got my first experience with a workstation computer, one I could see, touch, and even carry, an Apple Mac.

The computer was unlike any of the three mainframes I'd never seen, while the CAD software was unlike any I've seen since, with users "building" everything with configurable 6-sided virtual blocks. The maker of the pricey software gifted each of us a copy, asking us to return the favor by providing them with feedback - tips, tricks, shortcuts, bugs, etc. I couldn't believe my good fortune - after 20-plus years in school, after all the tuition I'd paid, now I was being paid in software… to play with blocks!

"Computers… are the greatest things… ever."

Two years later, computers I once swore "NEVER AGAIN!" would I use, I was teaching, to students at United Arab Emirates University, and I did so for 14 more years. Those computers I once swore "NEVER AGAIN!" would I use helped me earn a comfortable living and retire early. That's why I smile about my early experiences with computers… now.

039

YOUR SHOELACES ARE UNTIED

Count to ten. Tell time. Recite the ABCs. Why I even knew what day it was on a calendar. Yessiree, I could do all the kindergarten aptitude tests with ease, but that didn't seem to matter, what with my shoelaces untied unless some adult tied them for me. Then there was Petey, the teacher's pet. Sure, he knew how to tie his shoelaces, but I wasn't impressed, not with his frequently pee-soaked pants because he'd yet to master that skill. I thought his was the more serious problem than my untied shoelaces, but judging by the reactions I witnessed from orbiting adults... I was wrong.

Never before had I experienced the pressure to perform, to conform, the first stressors in my life put there by adults because I was neither performing nor conforming on that one simple thing - tying my shoelaces. Adults who should've known better mocked my lack of development and shamed me for lagging behind my younger classmates. One even thought my unruly laces were a sign of brain damage.

To start kindergarten in Eau Claire public schools, a student had to turn five years old before September 1. I turned five on September 2, so I had to wait another year. Numerous studies and anecdotal evidence claim boys trail girls in development by about a year, so in the overall scheme of things, having to wait likely set me up for success in school. And held back, I got another year of all-day recess, running around with my shoelaces untied, so what did I care?

Once I started school though, up to a year older than my classmates, perhaps those orbiting adults expected more from me. In contrast, my classmates didn't care if my shoes were untied. I'm not sure they even noticed, like Petey, when he needed to go to the little boy's room.

Even untied, my shoes stayed on my feet just fine, thank you, and if I wanted to take my shoes off, you know, in case of a sock emergency, there was no delay. I've never liked wearing shoes, figuring if Nature meant for me to wear them, I would've been born wearing socks - imagine the horror had they been a mismatched pair.

Another reason was that I've never had much patience for doing what doesn't interest me. Why I sought work that, for the most part, let me do what I wanted, even enjoyed, like piloting the Chief Waupaca. Instead of performing some soul-sucking job to help pay for college, I latched onto one that allowed me to toot a horn and ring a bell while wearing a captain's hat like the Skipper on the TV show Gilligan's Island.

Don't think I didn't take some flak for sticking with that job for ten seasons, at least twice as long as most thought I should've. Yet, what do I remember in my old(er) age? What do I write about? My time as Captain John. Would you rather read stories of me interning at an architect's office? Would I remember them? Would there even be any stories worth remembering? Still, the way too many treated me, it was like my untied shoelaces all over again.

I still don't like tying shoelaces. I feel the same about shaving, brushing my teeth, and trimming my finger and toenails. I do them, for obvious reasons, but each task takes time from my life that I'll never get back. One reason I retired at 44 was to be free to do what I wanted, not what someone else wanted. Even so, there are still daily performance reviews, but I conduct them, and the only expectations I must meet are my own.

"What?" …and sometimes Sue's.

"What?" …always Sue's.

Another reason I like being retired and living in remote locations is that I can more easily avoid the kinds of people who hounded me over my untied shoelaces. I didn't want those people in my life then, and I sure don't want them around now. Such people were hard to ignore when I was six and proved even harder to ignore as a working adult, society doing its darnedest to beat outliers into submission.

Starting with, apparently, the first day of kindergarten. How many kids dread going to school because others see them as different, make them feel ashamed, and pressure them to perform and conform? Even I'm guilty because I once told our dog, Packers, "No one is going to take you seriously until you start wearing pants," even though he and I both knew he never would. Well, I knew.

It seems as though there's always some adult around to criticize kids for coloring outside the lines or not tying their shoelaces soon enough. The criticism I faced seemingly every day until the day I tied, without thinking, the belt of my blue flannel robe and then applied the technique to my shoelaces. Even so, I untied them and waited for the next adult to chastise me for my untied laces. I didn't have to wait long…

"Your shoelaces are untied."

Without saying a word, I bent over and tied my laces, both shoes, then stood up, "There! They're tied." Back then, I wish I'd had the vocabulary to say, "Now piss off!"

I didn't like tied shoelaces, but I tied my shoes from that day forward because I didn't like people telling me my laces were untied even more. Nowadays, most days, you'd find me wearing nothing more than socks, sometimes mismatched, yet somehow life goes on, and around our house anyway, life is good.

Years after kindergarten came Velcro shoes, along with bread machines, calculators, microwave dinners, and self-driving cars. I'm happy I know how to tie my shoelaces, bake bread the old-fashioned way, do long division with paper and pencil, cook on a stovetop with pots and pans, and parallel park. Still, no one ever criticized me for being unable to do any of these things before I knew how, except for tying my shoelaces.

Not every popcorn kernel pops at the same time, so if there's a child-year-old in your life, please don't pressure them to perform and conform, especially to your expectations and timetable or that of others. If untied shoelaces are their only "problem," let them be. Like me, they'll probably figure it out when they have nothing better to do. If they don't, untied shoelaces will probably be the least of their problems.

040

SUE'S MOM

After Sue and I dated long enough that we felt we could vacation together in another country without causing an international incident, we planned a trip to Thailand for our 2003 summer break. Sue, always one to find unusual accommodations, reserved a hut that made me think we'd be staying on *Gilligan's Island* instead of Samui Island (Ko Samui), Thailand.

The hut was right on the beach. Right. On. The. Beach. Literally, fall off the thatched-roof covered porch and into the ocean close. Sue, who loves elephants even more than I do, also added a side trip to an "effelump" orphanage in the north of the country near Chang Mai. You can imagine our anticipation.

Then, just days before our departure, came the telephone call. I happened to be in Sue's flat at the time. Don't know why I would've been there because it was illegal for us to be alone together, in her flat, in Sharjah, in the United Arab Emirates. Nevertheless, there we were, alone together, in her flat, in Sharjah, in the United Arab Emirates.

Such a late-night call was not unexpected because months before, doctors diagnosed Sue's father, Art, with cancer, his prognosis grim. Having not yet met Sue's father, I was disappointed, knowing how much I wished Sue and Del could've met but never would - he dying thirteen years before she and I met. At least I'd gotten to speak with Art on the telephone.

While the trip to Thailand would be our first vacation as a couple, we'd already started traveling together over our summer break when we headed west from the United Arab Emirates to North America and then back. On the way over, we'd fly together as far as we could before splitting up - I then headed to Waupaca while Sue continued on to Calgary.

Separated by a time zone, an international border, and 1250 miles, I'd call a few times each week because Sue told me to, as calling showed I cared, or something like that. But when I called, most often it was not Sue, but Art who answered the telephone. A retired contractor, Art, and his crew, dug most of the basements in the Haysbro neighborhood of Calgary, including his own. So, in a house he helped build, the only home he'd known since 1958, old-school Art, in his house, answered his phone.

"Hello. Helderweirt's."

"Hello, Mr. Helderweirt, is Sue home?"

I'm sure her other love interests had asked Art the question many, many times, starting when Sue turned teenager because fathers were the original call screeners, the caller IDers. It's what old-school dads did if they had a daughter, especially an attractive one. What most teenage daughters never realized was that before making the call, the young man would rehearse a conversation with his hoped-for honey, agonizing over every word, sentence, question, and answer, trying to get it just right to make the best possible impression.

Then they had to work up the courage to actually make the call - mouth dry, hands sweaty, just thinking about dialing the number. With a big gulp and a "Here goes" dial, they would, eventually, the phone ringing, their heart pounding, the tension building... and then... the father would answer.

Never imagining anyone else would, despite all the rehearsal, they'd stutter and stammer as they spoke with the girl's father off script. What most young men never realized was it didn't matter if they said all the right things, nor did it matter how politely they said them, because all any father ever heard was, "I want to violate your daughter in a dozen different ways."

"Nope, Sue's not here," Art informed me.

"Of course not. She never is. No doubt out with her friends again," thoughts I kept to myself. Even though Art always answered, Sue's mother, a telephone operator until 1965 when she decided to become a stay-at-home mom, invariably got on the line.

"Hi, John!"

I never called Patricia by name. It was always, "Hi, Sue's Mom!"

Having not yet met, you might expect our conversations to have been an agonizing grind of awkward chitchat separated by even more awkward silence. They were not. The two of us happily got to know one another over the phone, our conversations sometimes lasting half an hour, international long distance.

One thing we talked about was how much we looked forward to meeting. I, because I knew Sue was "the one." Patricia, I think, I hope, because she knew I was "the one" for her daughter. Why else would Sue's Mom make such an effort to speak with me, especially since Sue told me her mother hadn't always approved of her choices in men? Including her first husband, Warren.

"Wait! What? Sue! You were married before?"

"Yes."

The things I learn fact-checking these stories...

So when the phone rang that late night in Sue's flat, we looked at each other with an unspoken but knowing trepidation that this might be "the call," the one where Sue's Mom would tell Sue her father was dying of cancer... or worse. Instead, the call was from Art. A moment of relief we'd been wrong shattered when he told Sue that after stepping out to the grocery store, he returned home to find Patricia lying on the bedroom floor.

Sue's Mom and I would never meet.

041

THE PARTING OF THE BLACK SEA

Shaking in her shoes, she was.

"Am I the reason why?"

Since I'd never had that effect on a woman, that I was aware of, I wasn't sure, so I stepped back. Her shaking stopped. So I stepped forward. Her shaking resumed. So I stepped back and stayed back, wishing I could ask, without creating a scene, why she was so afraid... of me.

Even though I taught on the Men's Campus during my first year at United Arab Emirates University, my first experience with students was on the Women's Campus. (A coincidence her name was) Shaikha and I, along with 24 other students, were in a classroom - I administering the placement exam they were taking. A listening exam, the soon-to-be first-year students answered questions based on my spoken English.

Owing to an overabundance of air conditioning inside to counter an overabundance of heat outside, I had trouble speaking, my mouth as dry as the dusty desert surrounding the campus. How dry was Al Ain? I didn't own a clothes dryer because I didn't need one. My bath towels were mainly for show. Dehydration landed some new colleagues in the hospital within 24 hours of arrival. And once, I didn't see it rain in Al Ain on the desert plain for six years.

My first time alone in a roomful of women, dressed in black from head to toe, and with no teaching experience, nerves also contributed to my case of cottonmouth. Years of teaching Muslim women later, every now and then in a classroom, the realization of where I was, what I was doing, and who my students were would hit me. Just for a couple-two-three seconds, as if someone pressed my Pause button, I'd look around the room... "Surreal..." ...and then I'd be right back at it, as if someone pressed my Play button, I once again feeling like I was where I was meant to be.

As for Shaikha, our close encounter may have been the first time since puberty she'd been adjacent to any male outside her immediate family, maybe the first time she'd seen a Western man up close. With blue eyes and fair skin, I surely looked different from most, if not all, the men she'd ever seen in person. Even my dress was different. In stark contrast to Emirati men who almost always wore all-white dishdashas, I stood too close for her comfort wearing a pair of baby-blue Bugle Boy chinos, a matching baby-blue and white striped seersucker shirt, and, decorated with colorful *Laugh-In* style hippie flowers, a woven blue cotton necktie that looked more like a sock.

My first necktie job, wearing even a stylish noose to work every day, particularly in the extreme heat of Al Ain, took some getting used to. So, too, did working around Muslim women as just getting to the exam room proved an unexpected challenge, the hallway outside literally wall-to-wall with students waiting for teachers to arrive. With the "Black Sea" between me and where I needed to be, at the end of the hall, I saw no way to get there - any physical contact with female students, even with their express written consent, strictly prohibited.

At that moment, I don't know if I ever felt more like the new guy, not only new to the job but also to teaching, the country, and the culture. As I stood there pondering my predicament, Tridib, a colleague with a valuable year of experience on the Women's Campus, must've surmised my situation, uttering under his breath as he passed behind me, "Just start walking, Mister John."

"Thanks, Tridib."

14 years later, we would cross paths again at Dubai Women's College, Tridib applying for a teaching job at the UAE's Higher Colleges of Technology. Monica, the woman who would be his supervisor, asked me about him before bidding on Tridib in the system's Byzantine hiring process after noticing our overlapping experience at UAEU.

"We didn't work on the same campus, so I can't tell you much."

"Anything would be helpful."

"Well, he was intelligent, articulate, and knows the deal teaching in the UAE."

"OK… good…"

Sensing she was disappointed I didn't offer more, I added, "There are people I worked with at the university I would definitely tell you not to hire… Tridib isn't one of them."

That recommendation made her smile, perhaps helping Tridib get the job. After he started work, he stopped by my cubicle and said, "Mister John! Thanks for putting in a good word for me!"

"Tridib! Mafi mushkallah!" and it was no problem because what I said was true, those the qualities I saw in him after only a short time at UAEU. Why, when the

Black Sea in front of me said I shouldn't, but Tridib said I should, I started walking...

Lo and behold, the Black Sea parted like the Red Sea. Even the ladies with their backs to me knew to step out of the way and in what direction to do so as if moved by an unseen force. After wading in a few steps, the Black Sea surrounded, an arm-length bubble separating me from certain trouble. As I made my way down the hall, so too did the bubble, opening in front of me as it closed behind me.

Biblical? I don't know about that, but at the time, it was one of the most miraculous things I'd ever seen... "Holy Moses!" Nevertheless, like finding out how a magician performs a trick, the "Moses Magic" was lost when I realized the parting of the Black Sea was due to a most subtle exchange of eye darts, head bobs, hand flicks, and barely audible verbal cues amongst the ladies. Still, I'll never forget my "Moses" moment.

After the exam, I provided a good laugh telling the tale to colleagues with Women's Campus experience. They then advised me not to abuse my "bubble power," explaining that while the ladies were responsible for steering clear of male faculty on the move, I was to give them every opportunity to do so. I should not walk in a way that would force them to walk into other students, faculty, furniture, doors, walls, trashcans, fountains, bushes, trees, poles, parked cars, moving traffic... or a men's restroom.

"I'll see what I can do."

Of course, female faculty didn't possess bubble power on the Women's Campus. In fact, they had a more difficult time than you might expect - female students not eager to make way for another woman. So while my path was always the one of least resistance, female colleagues had to navigate the Black Sea with incessant chatter, "Excuse me, pardon me, excuse me, coming through…"

But it didn't take long for new female faculty to figure out that bubble power could work for them, too… if they followed in the wake of a male colleague who was going their way…

"Miss Janet, three steps behind, please!"

"Just start walking, Mister John!"

042

MY HAPPY PLACE

My boss hated to see me coming.

That the case, most people would start looking for another job, but with my boss Pat, my job Captain John, and I not most people, I didn't need to update my resume. Pat, a macro manager, preferred never to see me, happy as long as the paperwork and payment for the charter the night before were in the cash register in the morning after he wandered over from his home across the road.

While the water side of the business was taking off, he preferred to concentrate on the land side - the also rapidly expanding bar and restaurant business. At night, after a charter, I'd usually see him hanging out outside, on the back deck, with customers, beer in hand, generally having a good time.

From his vantage point, he could see the Chief Waupaca pulling into the dock. If he didn't see me that night, he knew there were no problems. If, however, he spotted a man approaching wearing navy pants, a white shirt with epaulets, and a captain's hat, there'd be an owner with growing anxiety, a "How much is this going to cost me?" jolt back to reality, he figuring his good time over.

Until Pat replaced the Chief's old Gray Marine engine with a new Cummins diesel, some nights, it was. That Gray Marine chose the worst times to die, like when it was needed most - heading through a narrow channel into a whitecap-creating headwind, in the middle of an after-dark dinner charter with a boatload of seniors, or while shifting into reverse, the only way to stop the stern wheel paddleboat, you know, from crashing into the dock.

"HOLD ON!" most passengers figuring out why I'd shouted what I shouted one <THUD> too late, my warning coming at the last second. Maybe two, but I only had a second more after the engine went silent, the paddle still.

For more nights than we preferred following a charter, Pat and I stood at the edge of the engine compartment watching one of his on-call mechanics beer-belly deep in grease until the problem was no more. The long nights were necessary because the Chief had to be working for the first public tour at 11:30 the following morning. Pat never wanted to cancel tours as some people and groups traveled a long way for a boat ride, and he didn't want them to go away disappointed.

In my first year, Pat and I spent many nights together, not at the edge of the engine compartment but in the pilothouse. Pat accompanied me on all the nighttime charters because, as the new guy, I'd yet to prove myself. He wanted to make sure I knew what to do, especially when dealing with customers, as most nights, I would be not only the captain but also the crew, even with over 100 passengers onboard, often rowdy, intoxicated passengers.

Knowing I was unfamiliar with the 8 of the 22 Chain O'Lakes the Chief could navigate, Pat also wanted to make sure I knew where I was going, especially in the dark. While many of the glacial lakes were plenty deep, the hazards were many, with shallow, narrow channels that needed to be navigated along with several sand bars, rocks, and drunken boaters to be avoided.

As the season progressed and Pat's trust in me grew, he was not looking over my shoulder so much as sleeping on the pilothouse's back bench. When he was confident enough to let me pilot nighttime charters solo, it came with a solemn reminder, one I always kept in mind, "As captain of the Chief Waupaca, you are the face of my business, not me."

Even though I was hired part-time, I got a lot of face time, Pat and Mimi always finding work for me, although never as much as I created, so much so I almost always collected overtime with my pay. During the first few weeks of work, I spent each morning cleaning the bar, restaurant, and grounds, and then, along with Rita - hired to do daytime public tours - there were piloting lessons from Patty aboard the Chief.

The lessons, which went on for most of May, could get tedious with the heavy focus on docking, the most challenging part of piloting, especially when it was windy. The lessons were still my favorite part of the day, I not only aboard the Chief but spending time with the pretty and personable Patty. Why, after three weeks on the job, I was disappointed to discover she was already married… on the very day I'd worked up the courage to ask her out on a date, but before I did so. If I hadn't, that probably would've been its own story.

There was more to the Chief than just piloting, though, as there was the tour spiel. While I would eventually learn to pilot the Chief better than even Pat, I would never come close to matching Patty's shtick when it came to presenting public tours. Only once, visiting Universal Studios in Hollywood, did I hear anyone who could compare.

After lunch, for two weeks anyway, I was off to a home on Round Lake, not quite halfway down the Chain. The summer home belonged to Pat's parents, Dr. Pearse and Jane. My work there had nothing to do with the Chief or the Harbor Bar and Restaurant. Instead, Pat tasked me with turning a fallen tree into firewood for his parent's fireplace.

Before returning to the Harbor late in the afternoon for more piloting lessons with Patty, I spent a couple-two-three hours chainsawing and chopping, chainsawing and chopping, chainsawing and chopping, then stacking the firewood between two still-standing trees between the house and the water's edge. No one ever checked on me, but Mimi was all smiles one Monday morning as she approached. Over the weekend, she and Pat had stopped by the house on Round Lake to check on my progress. Mimi was most impressed with my wood-stacking ability.

"It's so neat. How do you do that?"

"My Grandpa Curran taught me."

"Thank your Grandpa Curran."

"I will."

It wasn't what I expected, but it was outside work, unsupervised, and with a view of Round Lake. Hired to pilot a sternwheel paddleboat, something I'd never done on lakes I'd hardly ever been on, chopping and stacking firewood was something I knew well, getting me off to a good start in my new but unrelated job as Captain John.

When it came to the Chief, though, almost everything was a new experience. I didn't know about many things Pat told me to do, but I figured them out. Usually. Over time, many of the maintenance jobs that were Pat's became mine, like greasing the bearings, most accessed via small hatches that opened into fittingly small compartments below the lower deck. That I could "bend it like Gumby" came in handy in those claustrophobic spaces, where I learned that doing what no one else wanted to do was good for job security.

Whenever possible, I found ways to make such jobs fun, like greasing the drive chains for the paddle. I'd gunk what I could reach, then climb on the paddlewheel, walking it, using the paddles as steps, like one bitching bright-red StairMaster, moving the paddle, and the chains, to get the sections out of reach within reach. I never found a way to make pumping sewage fun, though. That job was what it was - I happy when none ended up on the boat, the dock, the lake… or me.

Pat wasn't the only one who jumped aboard to observe me during my first season. So what could be worse than the boss looking over my shoulder? How about the boss's mother? Especially after I asked Jane for her ticket as she boarded for a daytime tour on Rita's day off. Jane replied, rather curtly, "I don't need one." That was the awkward circumstance in which I met Pat's mother.

A smoker, Jane always wanted an ashtray. Stored in a cabinet inside the pilothouse, I only put them out at night for charters because Pat wanted to discourage smoking on the boat during daytime tours and didn't allow it in the lower enclosed portion of the boat anyway. Grudgingly, I'd give Jane an ashtray… and then she'd happily give me a lecture on how she shouldn't have to ask for one.

"Talk to your son!"

As difficult as the boss's mother could be, I knew what to expect, at least when it came to ashtrays. Such was not the case with the stone-faced Pearse. It took some time, but like my Grandpa Curran, I learned he was a good guy, once you got to know him, if you got to know him, because his gruff exterior encouraged people to leave him alone. So I treated Pearse like my Grandpa Curran, and we got along just fine.

When Pearse and Jane were aboard, I knew they weren't just along for the ride. They were there to spy on me, to see how I handled the passengers and presented the tour because I had no supervision once I backed out of the dock. That first season, they kept me on my toes, not only with their presence but also with their "presence."

Even Patty snuck aboard to spy a time or two, hiding between tours in a lower deck bathroom while I compared tickets collected versus tickets sold with Therese, "Queen of the Ticket Booth." And she was. Made one heck of an ice cream cone, too. If I had a dollar for every passenger who asked me if that good-looking redhead in the ticket booth was my wife, I could've afforded more ice cream cones.

With me, apparently, sharing the dispositions of both my Grandpa Curran and Pearse, Therese was always telling me, "Smile, John Boy!" Her "nagging" got me to smile more, though, and over the years, even after Therese moved on, I found it easier to do and that it didn't cost me anything.

That first season, the more I did, the more I did well, the more Pat gave me to do, and the more he trusted me to get it done. While I was learning on the job, so too was Pat, he getting to know his new boat captain. One thing Pat was pleased to discover was that I didn't drink alcohol… then. The last thing he wanted was a customer filing an insurance claim, especially if his boat captain had alcohol on their breath. Even though Pat never recouped any of my paychecks at the bar, he didn't mind, knowing the hardest drink his captain drank while piloting was water on the rocks.

Eventually, they stopped spying on me, figuring the new guy no longer was. Instead, I was "the guy" because, for that season and the next nine, I missed only one nighttime charter - the day Dan and Marsha got married. The last summer before Pat purchased a second boat, a custom-built motor yacht I never had much use for (it lacked the Chief's character and was too easy to drive), there was a stretch where I piloted for charters 13 nights in a row. On two of those nights, I did two three-hour charters, my longest day some 14 hours behind the Chief's massive wheel. I loved the job so much, though. Even more on payday, I never working the part-time for which I was hired.

By the end of my rookie season, I'd settled into the job, one I worked hard to define, knowing I'd found something special, an opportunity like no other. To this day, I can't imagine what else I would've done in those ten seasons that would've been as rewarding. More importantly, though, in a town where I always felt like an outsider, I finally found a home - I was who I was supposed to be, Captain John, where I was supposed to be, aboard the Chief Waupaca - my happy place.

043

OL' WHAT'S HIS NAME

The military called it a Canadian Forces Station. The locals called it The Elephant Pen. I know which moniker I prefer. Centered in a quarter-mile square clearing just east of Masset, British Columbia, what appeared to be two fences encircled the expressionless building block, about 150 feet on a side. The outer fence, about 300 yards in diameter, really was a fence, chain link, topped by barbed wire, but the inner "fence," about 250 yards in diameter, gave the installation its nickname. Four times higher than the surrounding fence, what it really was was a Wullenweber AN/FRD-10 Circularly Disposed Antenna Array (CDAA).

Elephant Pen it is.

Sandwiched between North Beach and Tow Hill Road, the antenna, erected in 1971 to locate and classify enemy ships and submarines, is still operational even though the military hasn't stationed anyone there since 1997. Another CFS, located just south of Ottawa, Ontario, operates the site remotely for the benefit of the Canadian Forces Intelligence Branch.

The Elephant Pen isn't the only remnant of the town's Cold War history, as much of Masset's housing consists of former Private Married Quarters (PMQs), military housing for those who manned the outpost. The military constructed these two-story single homes and two-story duplexes around a series of ten cul-de-sacs, each loop given the name of a tree - Pine, Spruce, Maple, Hemlock, Alder, Balsam, Fir, Elm, Cedar, and Dogwood. Now privately owned, most houses, including ours on Dogwood, retain their original "charm," but a few homeowners have renovated to differentiate their box from others in their "Q-patch."

While I found the cloak-and-dagger installation interesting - I must admit when first faced with the massive circular antenna, donning a tinfoil hat didn't seem so crazy - it was but a quirky diversion on the way to Masset's top attraction, North Beach. Stretching east then northeast for 25 uninterrupted miles from Masset to Rose Spit, the beach attracts tourists and locals alike.

You know those Caribbean beaches with the powdery white sand, tranquil azure seas, swaying palm trees, and ever-pleasant temperatures? You won't find any of that on North Beach. You know what else you won't find? Cabana boys serving froofy drinks with tiny umbrellas to well-oiled tourists in flip-flops lounging on oversized beach towels in undersized bathing suits.

No one's ever going to confuse North Beach with those that front Caribbean resorts. For one, swaying palms don't back North Beach, but a lush, temperate, not tropical rainforest because the beach is fairly far north. How far north? On a clear day, you can see Alaska, so the temperature seldom rises above 70F, even in the summer. And, as the name implies, North Beach faces north into the wind that blows off the chilly and often choppy waters of the Dixon Entrance.

As a part of Art's master plan, we arrived in Masset in early July, right smack in the middle of the crabbing season. As you might expect, when we first arrived on North Beach, it was overrun. Scanning the surf as far as the eye could see, counting Sue, Art, Scott, Joanne, and myself, I counted six crabbers that day.

Dressed in layers to delay the onset of hypothermia - "Ah, summer in Canada!" - no suntan lotion was required, but chest waders were as the crabs were under the surf. As we headed into the crashing waves, fishnets in hand, we looked like a Special Forces team... in an alternate bizarro universe. Sue and I didn't know what to expect, as we'd never been crabbing. Yet, there we were, just four days removed from the stifling summer heat of the United Arab Emirates, up to our armpits in chest waders, layered in clothes, chasing crabs off a beach conveniently located to the North Pole.

Peering under the waves, it was difficult just spotting a crab, and they had the advantage of seeing me, or at least my legs, before I saw them. After I located one, even with their drunken sailor walk, those little buggers could move, often scurrying away before I could get my net into position. Once I got the hang of it, though, I caught one. Then there was the struggle to get the crab out of the net, its many appendages tangled in the nylon mesh. Having freed it from the net, you'd think it would've been grateful. Instead, it pinched one of my fingers, hard.

"SONOFABITCH! You little..."

After cursing a crab that was only trying to defend itself, there was the frustration in determining that the crab I'd worked so hard to catch... was just a smidge too small to keep.

"ARGH!"

I knew because a homemade measuring device was strung around each of our necks, sort of a U-shaped wooden block. A crab was too small if the widest part of its shell could fit between the legs of the U. That crab fit, barely, and there was just no way to make its shell any wider than it was. So, despite my throbbing finger, I had to put the crab back where I found it.

"Next year, you little…"

Even though I'd only managed to catch a couple keepers, I'd had an unexpectedly good time matching wits with the crabs. The chase was the thing for me, but I was disappointed knowing Art couldn't fill his freezer with my fun. I felt better after returning to shore and discovering no one else had done any better, including Art. My relief was his anguish and it only intensified because our luck was even worse the next few days, crabbing out of the question - the water simply too rough.

Instead, Art went fishing with Scott on his boat. Sue and I wanted to go, but our time was limited, so we skipped the fishing trips. Intrigued by the islands, we wanted to see more of Haida Gwaii, taking the opportunity to explore on land while Art and Scott were on the water. We did not need to tag along as any fish they caught could go on our licenses so long as they didn't exceed their limit on any given day.

Art didn't have a passport in his later years, and purposely so. He didn't see the need as his annual trip to Haida Gwaii was as far as he cared to venture. That summer, with Sue and me joining him, he hauled a chest freezer and a generator all the way from Calgary, hoping that with the addition of our licenses, collectively, we could catch enough seafood to make the extra effort worthwhile.

Unfortunately for Art, the fishing those first few days was no better than the crabbing. What we caught wouldn't have filled a Coleman cooler, much less his jumbo chest freezer. Art was not a happy man, absolutely beside himself that the weather was not cooperating. In the evenings, seated around the dinner table, we could've cut the tension with a knife, it's not like we needed it to cut up crab or filet fish.

A nearly empty freezer wasn't the only thing aggravating Art because shortly after we arrived in Masset, everyone noticed he was increasingly unhappy... with me. Except for me, as I just assumed Art was a crabby old man, he often referring to me as "Ol' What's His Name," harumph included.

After cluing me in, Sue asked, "What did you say?"

"Nothing... as far as I know."

I'd met Art in person two years previous, just a month after his wife and Sue and Scott's mother, Patricia, unexpectedly passed away from complications of an undiagnosed cancer. However, this was the first time Art and I had spent any quality time together. Confined in his pickup truck for over 20 hours on the drive from Calgary to Prince Rupert, we didn't have much choice.

Sue eventually learned the reason for Art's inexplicable behavior. Seems he was upset because he saw Sue paying for everything, while my wallet stayed in my pocket. I couldn't fault Art for that, especially since he saw what there was to see, he just looking out for his daughter. If anyone understood that, I did.

What Art didn't realize was that Sue and I were already working as a team, even if it wasn't obvious. Living in the same apartment building near the Dubai/ Sharjah border, we agreed that when we headed north toward Sharjah, Sue would drive, but when we headed south toward Dubai, I would drive.

Traveling in the States and Canada, we had a similar arrangement. When we headed north to Canada, Sue drove and paid, and when we headed south to the States, I drove and paid. But Art only saw Sue's half of our agreement and thought I was taking advantage of his daughter... and he didn't like that. Even though Sue straightened him out, I think he still didn't know what to make of me. After all, I was an American... and you know how those people are.

When the weather finally improved, so did the fishing and Art's mood. He was satisfied with the catch of salmon and halibut, and the crabbing improved, although we were still far from reaching our crustacean limit. Running out of time to meet our quota, we all felt pressure to produce.

On the final day, though, everyone was catching crab, I having a particularly good day, catching keepers left and right. Every now and then, I'd snare a pair of mating crabs, much easier to catch when they're "occupied," they not even seeming to notice or mind. However, if one was too small to keep (the females generally larger than the males), I had to pull them apart... they then... crabby.

Crabby or not, on this day, it was all about getting them into the net. With the surf still somewhat rough, Art stayed on the beach, preferring instead to organize the collection and storage of the crab for the ride back to Masset. With each full net, I waded to shore, beaming, knowing the smile I'd put on Art's face... and Sue's.

I caught more than anyone that day, helping fill Art's freezer with as much crab as our licenses allowed. There was a massive sense of relief that Art would need the freezer and the generator to haul our catch back to Calgary. More importantly, for me anyway, sometime that day, I think Art decided "Ol' What's His Name" wasn't such a bad guy after all.

o44

EVEN THE CHICKEN COMPLAINED

"Gringos!"

The wave of Western expats that would flood Ecuador had yet to arrive in July 2006, so Sue and I stood out in the crowd. Just outside the international arrivals terminal at the Quito airport, it was crowded, with hoards of overeager taxi drivers wanting to take us for a ride. No doubt a few wanted to really take us for a ride, but we had no need of a taxi, yet.

Instead, we had to make our way to the national terminal for our flight to Loja, the airport nearest to Vilcabamba. We soon discovered that to get to the national terminal, we had to squeeze our way past the taxi drivers grabbing at our bags to take us on a ride we didn't need, and walk a block down the street. While not impressed, we'd seen worse airport arrangements... talking to you, Charles De Gaulle - the airport, not the former French president it's named for.

Once inside the Quito national terminal, we checked in at the TAME counter, the then-national airline of Ecuador. Really. Nice. People. Some spoke English well enough, even I could understand. While we couldn't purchase our tickets online, a TAME customer service agent I emailed from Dubai assured me our reservation would be waiting for us, we'd just have to pay when we collected our boarding passes. As promised, that's precisely what happened.

There were two daily return flights from Quito to Loja - after sunrise and before sunset. Arriving too late from Panama for the first, Sue and I spent the afternoon waiting for the second. At least it gave us a chance to catch our breath after a whirlwind month that started with our epic three-day journey from Dubai to Haida Gwaii.

When the boarding call finally came, we were directed to exit through a door and directly onto the tarmac. We walked past a lineup of other planes, some with propellers, some without, ours parked at the far end. "No props!" so Sue was happy. As we climbed the portable staircase, entered the cabin, and took our seats, we noticed Ecuadorians boarded the plane as they'd done for the flight from Panama City to Quito - as if it were a church with wings, the process all so civilized.

The flight path from Quito to Loja takes passengers down the spine of the Andes Mountains, in particular, over the Avenida de los Volcanes (Avenue of the Volcanoes). Mainland Ecuador has 28 volcanoes, so far, and on a clear day, many of them are visible on the 50-minute flight between Quito and Loja. Even on cloudy days, sometimes the snow-capped peaks poke through the clouds.

On this day, we were fortunate to see Volcan Tungurahua, Quechua for "Throat of Fire." It had just started a period of violent activity only a few days before. Eye-popping color photos of the fiery eruptions graced the front pages of the newspapers we saw at the Quito airport upon our arrival - Welcome to Ecuador! Flying past the angry volcano, I thought the plane would list to the left as everyone on the right side got up to look out the erupting side. Fortunately, we were already seated on the action/adventure half of the plane.

On our final approach to the Loja airport, the pilot made a sharp U-turn. Looking down, we no longer saw any volcanoes, but we didn't see any place even remotely flat enough to land a plane. As the pilot completed the U-turn, we descended into a narrow mountain valley. All we saw to our left was mountain. All we saw to our right was mountain. "OK. The pilot knows what he's doing. Sure he does."

A couple of minutes later, we saw the runway out a right side window... just as the pilot made a hard right turn, emphasis on hard. So sharp was the turn, all we saw to our left was blue sky, and all we saw to our right was a wondrous mosaic of lush green fields courtesy of the Catamayo River and a system of irrigation canals. I'd always thought the only reason airplanes had seatbelts was to make it easier for recovery crews to locate bodies after a crash, but on this approach, they actually helped keep us in our seats.

Upon completing the high-banked turn, the pilot immediately, emphasis on immediately, leveled out the plane, just in time to touch down with a planeload of cheering passengers, including Sue and me. As the plane taxied to the terminal, we noticed a gathering crowd behind a chain-link fence. Had they heard of our imminent arrival? Were they clamoring for a glimpse of the gringos from el Norte? Probably not. Even so, their enthusiasm was contagious as Sue and I realized we were now that much closer to our ultimate destination, Vilcabamba.

Before an extensive renovation, the old Loja Airport was small. For passengers, it was nothing more than a few big rooms and one small bathroom. So with just the one evening flight, it took no time to get in and out of the terminal, where, once again, overeager taxi drivers were there to greet us. Some offered us rides to Vilcabamba for $40, but we declined as it seemed pricey. Other drivers made other offers to take us to Catamayo or Loja, but we declined as all sounded on the high side.

Because of our last-minute change of plans, we didn't have time to research Ecuador as thoroughly as we normally would've done. During our negotiation for a taxi ride, we discovered that while our plane tickets said Loja, much to our surprise, we were not near Loja, but just outside the city of Catamayo.

"¿Dónde está Loja?"

"Allí," said the taxi driver, pointing east toward a distant mountain range.

"Cuánto tiempo?"

"45 minutos."

With the sun setting almost as rapidly as the taxi stand and terminal were emptying, we decided $5 was an acceptable fare for the ride to Loja, for no other reason than it was the last remaining taxi and we were the last remaining passengers. So we piled into the little yellow taxi, barely big enough for us, our two carry-on bags, and the driver.

Other than some beautiful mountain scenery and a nicely paved highway, there wasn't much between Catamayo and Loja. Oddly, it reminded me of the drive to Wisconsin from Chicago's O'Hare Airport, not because of the scenery, or the nicely paved highway, but because the locals drove like they were from Illinois.

Just outside of Catamayo, the driver asked us where we wanted to go in Loja. I think that's what he asked, I not using my Spanish for so many years, I wasn't sure. But asking where we wanted to go seemed like something a taxi driver would ask... in a taxi. The problem was, we didn't know, but before I could reply, he suggested, more than asked, "Terminal Terrestre."

Bus terminal? Sounds good to me. "Si, Señor."

It was dark by the time we arrived at the Loja bus terminal. No matter, as all we needed to do was find a bus to take us to Vilcabamba. Ecuador had buses going everywhere, so… "How hard could that be?"

I had to ask. We walked the terminal but couldn't find a bus to Vilcabamba, on the way to nothing more than a remote part of Ecuador… and a remoter part of Peru. "Hmmm… maybe we should've taken the offer of a pickup taxi ride to Vilcabamba for $40." Too late. We felt better declining the offer, later, after we learned the usual fare for the then 90-minute ride was only $30.

On our first meander through the terminal, we'd gone no further than the public toilets, figuring nothing could be beyond those. Nothing. The second time around, approaching desperate, we held our noses, and in the far back corner of the L-shaped terminal, we found the ticket office for the one and only bus line (at the time) that transported passengers to Vilcabamba.

"VilcabambaTuris!"

"Cuánto?" I inquired at the counter, never so happy to have the opportunity to buy a bus ticket. By then, the young lady behind the counter could've said any amount under a hundred dollars, and I would've said, "Dos, por favor."

She said, "Uno dollar."

I replied, "Dos, por favor."

With our tickets in hand, we passed through the turnstiles to the parking area and waited for our bus, which she said would arrive in ten minutes. At least, I think that's what she said. Maybe she said we wouldn't last ten minutes on the bus. I don't know. I was still trying to find my ear for Español.

Ten minutes or so later, though, as promised, the burgundy and silver VilcabambaTuris bus arrived empty, no one other than the driver getting off. OK, apparently, no one in Vilcabamba wanted to go to Loja. We found out later that those who do get off at stops closer to downtown before the bus reached the terminal on the far side of the city. We were also the only ones who boarded the bus. OK, apparently, no one in Loja wanted to go to Vilcabamba either. We were about to discover passengers got on the bus like they got off - anywhere but the terminal.

In the dark, we didn't see much on our ride around the edge of downtown Loja and saw even less on the ride to Vilcabamba because, away from the city lights, it was inside of a cow dark. Unfortunately, because in the daytime, the scenic mountain drive I never tire of would've been a great introduction to Vilcabamba. However, in the dark, we might as well have been crossing the Saskatchewan prairie, beautiful in a far more horizontal way.

Just over an hour later, we were the only ones who'd not gotten off the bus before it reached the terminal in Vilcabamba. For most of the trip, the bus was standing room only as passengers continued to pile on even though all the seats had long been occupied. "Cozy" it was. Even the chicken complained.

While the owner of the property we'd come to see had made a reservation for us at a local hostel, the Jardín Escondido (Hidden Garden), we had no idea where in Vilcabamba it was, which hardly mattered because we had no idea where in Vilcabamba we were. As Sue and I shared shrugs, we interrupted each other with a, "Now what?"

Looking over my shoulder, Sue spotted a large map painted on the wall of a building across the street from the bus station… a map to the Jardín Escondido! We walked across the street to check it out, learning our destination was six or so blocks away.

After arriving in Panama late the night before, meeting with an attorney in Panama City earlier that morning, then flying to Quito, then not Loja, followed by a taxi ride to Loja and the bus ride to Vilcabamba, we were more than tired. Spotting a little yellow taxi parked in the terminal, like the one we rode from Catamayo to Loja, we decided, with almost no discussion, to take a taxi to the Jardín instead of walking the blocks toting our carry-on bags.

A gentle wrap on the window woke the sleeping driver. In Spanish, I asked, as best I could, if he would give us a ride. "Sí." So we piled in, "Jardín Escondido, por favor." I figured since Vilcabamba was so small, he must know where the Jardín was, what with the giant map painted on the wall across the street.

However, it wasn't long before we realized we were heading out of town and back to Loja. We didn't know it then, but the little yellow taxis were only licensed to transport passengers between Loja and Vilcabamba. I guess he figured we knew that. We did not, but then he didn't know the English word "STOP!" but soon learned.

After some confusion, we eventually got him to turn around and take us back to the bus terminal. After paying the man for his trouble and apologizing profusely, we decided it might be easier to walk it, especially since we appeared to be the only ones out and about. With the sidewalks already rolled up for the night, even though it was only nine o'clock, we managed to find our way to the Jardín Escondido all right, only to find the front gate closed and locked.

"Ugh."

"Doorbell!"

<DING>

"I sure hope someone answers."

Someone did, eventually, and let us in. After getting checked in, we made our way to a second-floor room with a private bath... and a bed firmer than the sagging floor. I don't think we would've slept much that night anyway, not with what we hoped awaited us in the morning.

045

THE PLATONIC PAVILION

I. Was. Furious.

Furious. That's what I was. No, not over Professor Keegan's "Nice hat" remark. That was September, and it was now half past Halloween. Besides, Kent was right. I should've checked my nice hat at the door.

Furious. That's what I was, sitting alone in my dorm room, which by law could be smaller than a prison cell, but then I had the option to leave whenever I wanted.

Furious. That's what I was, staring at an almost blank dorm room wall. Almost because left from the previous night's drawing session was a failed technical pen stuck in the drywall.

Following Kent's remark during the roll call on the first day of my Architectural Fundamentals 200 class at the University of Wisconsin-Milwaukee, things got worse, bottoming out in November. ARCH200 was over for the week after yet another grueling day of critiques, and while Kent torpedoed my latest design, that's not why I was furious.

As we sat motionless during the two-hour class, Kent randomly, or so it seemed, would call out a name - the next presenter. None of us knew if we would be next... or last. It was nerve-wracking. How long can you hold your breath? I discovered I could hold mine for almost two hours because that day, I was last. Even so, after Kent called my name, he did what he did for no other student - he looked around the room to see who this John Curran guy was.

"Hey! Over here! It's me! Nice hat guy!" I shouted, to myself, furious he knew everyone in the class but not me.

"If you know all the others, I'm the one you don't know!" I shouted, once again to myself.

To be fair, I shared the blame for Kent's not knowing who I was because, other than wearing my nice hat to his class, I hadn't done anything to distinguish myself, especially when it came to the designs I tacked to the wall. For that, I was at least as furious with myself as I was with Kent.

My other classes and dinner provided some distraction for the remainder of the day, but that night, in my dorm room, I stewed in my pre-owned comfy chair purchased at the Purple Heart Value Village, then on North Avenue, for five dollars. I took note but passed on the pre-owned underwear I wouldn't have purchased at any price.

That I was furious wasn't necessarily a bad thing, as anger could inspire me. Sometimes, if I wasn't angry, I'd find a reason to be, to get my juices flowing. Maybe Kent pretended not to know who I was to inspire me, but that night, that thought never crossed my mind, nor would I have believed it if it had.

"Doesn't know who I am? I'll show him!" And I would because as the day disappeared, the light switched on, my anger replaced by an idea. Much as I wish I could, I can't explain how it happened, but I got "it," what Kent meant by integrated design, and then I got an idea, a design I'd be proud to tack to the wall come the next presentation day.

The entire semester, we worked on but one project, the Platonic Pavilion, celebrating Kent's version of Platonic solids - sphere, cube, pyramid, cone, and cylinder. His design briefs were precisely that, brief. To celebrate the solids, he didn't tell us much more than our pavilions were to include three zones - entry, transition, and gathering - the square footage of each was mostly irrelevant, as long as the design worked. Early on, we didn't even have a site plan.

Instead, we designed in a vacuum, on an imaginary plinth of infinite whiteness... or whatever fit on our drawing board. While it might seem easier, designing in a vacuum is more difficult because there's nothing to tell a designer what to do. Eventually, given a site plan - featuring hills, flats, and a water element - we could put our pavilion wherever we wanted. I knew just where to put my latest design for the pavilion, the first time all semester that I felt confident in what I was doing.

Struggling with just about anything new - wanting to know how all the pieces fit - I often fell behind the curve. But once I got it and understood how all the pieces fit, I really got it and put myself ahead of the curve. For the longest time, I thought it was just a "me" thing until a girlfriend told me her brother also wanted to know how all the pieces fit, so he too seemed dumb at first, but then when he got it, he made everyone else seem dumb.

So, no surprise, in ARCH200, I started slowly - my early designs met with apathy. When it comes to the product of any creative process I engage in, I want the response to my work to be "Love it," or even "Hate it," there nothing worse than "Meh." Subsequent critiques weren't any better, including the most recent, because after Kent looked around to see who I was, he likened my three-zone pavilion design to "Twins connected by an umbilical cord." Ouch. His comment cut like a Ginsu knife - as seen on TV.

Harsh? Yes, but his remark turned out to be the key that opened the door to my understanding of integrated design... once my anger subsided and I focused on what Kent said after not knowing who I was. So, while most students were out enjoying their Thursday night, sunk deep in my five-dollar chair, I drew my design for the pavilion in micro size, as always. I liked micro scale, even though it could hide problems because I could see the big picture without moving my eyes. I could see how all the pieces fit.

On presentation day, as I tacked my boards to the wall, even before I'd said a word, Kent was already smiling that satisfied smile a teacher gets when they see a student who's made a breakthrough. A smile I didn't fully appreciate then but did after I became a teacher. My presentation may have been the first time that semester the room relaxed, Kent's happiness over my design, that someone "got it," contagious.

Kent awarded me an A+ on the project and an A for the semester only because the university grading system did not permit grades of A+. Signing up for any subsequent class he taught that I could take, Kent was my professor for more classes in my six years at UWM. For every class except one (another story for another book), I earned, earned an A, something few other students did.

I didn't care what my grade was, though, because what mattered to me was how much I learned from Kent, inside and outside the classroom. He was the best teacher I ever had. Along the way, I hope he learned something from me besides my name.

I think then Professor (later Dean) Dr. Robert (Bob) Greenstreet explained why I liked Kent better than I could when he said, "Kent really was an exceptional teacher - his passion for education, coupled with his extraordinary breadth of knowledge, made him a compelling instructor and one who touched the lives of many alumni and students. He had the ability to make students reach deep inside themselves and come up with some startling work which they hitherto didn't know they were capable of doing."

I didn't know I was capable of doing what I did for the Platonic Pavilion project. Even now I shake my head and ask… "Did I do that?"

A licensed architect and engineer, Kent earned Master's degrees in both subjects at the University of Illinois. Still, his proudest accomplishment was winning a University Distinguished Teaching Award (known as the Amoco Good Teaching Award when Kent won it). The award recognizes excellence in teaching performance at the undergraduate level, in the classroom, the arena he most loved.

All these years later, the Platonic Pavilion is still my favorite design project from architecture school, even more than the project for my Master of Architecture thesis, chaired by Kent. My presentation boards were also the peak of my drawing skills. With neither my hands nor my eyes what they once were, I know I could never again produce three ink-on-whiteboard drawings like that, but then, I don't have to.

Integrated design became… a part of me… and a part of my thesis project, one I continue to work on as a hobby. Hired to develop a new CAD/Interior Design program for the United Arab Emirates Higher Colleges of Technology, my focus was integrated design. Tasked at Dubai Women's College with integrating projects from four departments - English, Math, Computers, and Business - into one project, my success made me the "Golden Boy," for a while anyway, as those projects became a model for the 13-campus HCT system.

Finally, for all the stories in this book series, "Like jigsaw puzzle pieces, once you start putting them together, you'll begin to see the big picture, the story of John's life unexpected," I purposely don't tell you what the big picture, the story of my life unexpected is. As in Kent's class, I want you to figure out how the pieces fit and what they mean, freeing you to find your answers.

046

WORLD'S LARGEST MEN'S CLUB

I don't have a figure for the ratio of males to females in Al Ain's gritty industrial area of Sanaiya, but it had to approach infinity because if you saw a woman there, she was probably lost, and not just in a directional sense.

Strange as it may sound, Al Ain and Platteville had a fair bit in common because if I got up high enough in either location, I could see the end of the world, just down the road. Both were make your own kind of fun places. And each suffered from a noticeable shortage of women, men everywhere in Al Ain. Everywhere. Especially in Sanaiya.

The vast majority of workers in the UAE were foreigners, like me, hired to do the jobs Emiratis could not, or would not do, locals just 10% of the population. Most, like me, were also men, populating nearly every shop, even if those shops sold ladies' clothing, including lingerie. In addition, men were the overwhelming majority in government offices, banks, the telephone company, post offices, and UAE University, where I taught. They drove every taxi, truck, and bus. They built every building and then cleaned those buildings. They built every street and then maintained those streets. They sold every car and then serviced those cars.

The only jobs where women were in significant numbers, occasionally a majority, were as teachers, nurses, wait staff, secretaries, supermarket checkers, hairdressers, cleaners, and household servants... similar to the United States... in 1953. In residential areas, the male-to-female ratio was better balanced simply because most foreign workers there were housemaids. I rarely saw the women they served, though, but then, moving to Al Ain at the end of July, I didn't see many people on the streets my first month, male or female, because of the searing heat.

That heat (the thermometer at my villa once read 134F... in the shade) even made a mountain disappear. As I'd done at the end of nearly every workday during my first month in Al Ain, I walked out the front gate of the Women's Campus to catch a taxi home. This time, though, I saw a mountain I'd not seen before.

"Where'd that come from?"

"It's always been there."

"You sure?"

Topping out at 4,098 feet, over 3,000 feet higher than the surrounding desert, Jebel Hafeet was the UAE's best-known peak, even if Jebel Jais, at 6,345 feet, was the country's highest. Located just eleven miles from campus, I'd not seen Jebel Hafeet because the summer heat and blowing sand, combined with smoke from the oil well fires post-Gulf War (the "Kuwait Cloud"), had cloaked it in an orangey-brown haze. Only a slightly cooler, calmer day in late August allowed me to see the mountain's still fuzzy profile.

Having missed seeing a nearby mountain for the better part of a month, I started paying more attention to my surroundings. The result? Just a few days later, I discovered girls. After backing out of my car park one morning, I saw young ladies here, there, everywhere...

dressed in blue and white nun-style uniforms, waiting for the school bus.

"Where'd they come from?"

"They've always been here."

"You sure?"

I never drove down the street more slowly than I did that first day of the new school year for K-12 students. The odd thing was, I never saw the girls return home, but I know they did because six mornings a week, there they were, waiting for the bus. Local families could be double-digit large, but they couldn't replace a half-dozen or more daughters so quickly. That could take years, maybe a couple-two-three more wives.

Except for the girls waiting for the bus every morning, the start of a new school year at UAE University meant I saw even fewer women, as I taught on the Men's Campus. There were, of course, no female students or female faculty - women, then, not allowed to teach men. Except for a few exceptions, only older and/or married men taught on the Women's Campus simply because there weren't enough female faculty.

Given the first thing told me on my first day at UAE University was, "You'll never teach on the Women's Campus," I never expected to work there. Before the start of my second year, though, that shortage of female faculty resulted in the director transferring me to the Women's Campus, even though I'd just turned 30 and was single.

One of the first unmarried Western men permitted to teach on the Women's Campus at UAEU was a major reason why I stayed for eight years, then returned for one semester at Sharjah Women's College, and then another six years at Dubai Women's College. I found interacting with the local women fascinating and teaching them far more rewarding, regarding each as an unexpected privilege… and… and… I got to work with female faculty and staff, like Sue. Not that there weren't any women working on the Men's Campus my first year, because there were, a few, and fewer still who were single.

In administration, there was Safina, from Nubia, a region along the Nile River straddling the border between Egypt and Sudan. Given her enormous size - big-boned she was - taller and far wider than me, orbiting astronauts could've spotted her, even when she was indoors, especially in her gaudy-in-a-good-way getups. Standing next to her waiting for an elevator was claustrophobic, never mind how I felt after we stepped inside - the old "Otis box" not much larger than a dumbwaiter.

There was Vivian, a fiery redhead from New York City. She never bothered to learn the local vernacular for left, right, and straight ahead, which came in handy in directing the mostly Pakistani taxi drivers around Al Ain. Instead, she just backhanded her driver on the shoulder and pointed. Maybe that's how she did it in The Big Apple.

I tried not to bother her unless I absolutely had to. Shuttered away most of the day and many a night in a walk-in closet of an office dealing with our balky computer network, she more than earned her pay doing a thankless job that made mine and every other faculty member's easier. Others did not show her the same courtesy though, including an upper management type who didn't know math as well as our students, harshly criticizing Vivian for her having to redo 40 of the over 4000 class schedules she'd generated. 40 of over 4000 - a 40% failure rate in his innumerate little mind.

There was Ghada, my Quran-gifting Egyptian friend. She grew up mainly in Arkansas and earned a computer science degree from the University of Minnesota-Duluth. I visited with Ghada regularly, the cubicle where she did her computer programming just down the hall from mine. She taught me a lot about a lot, helping me more than she ever knew, getting my expat life off to a good start. Now in Australia, I hope to thank her in person one day.

There were the two library assistants who rotated between the Men's and Women's campuses - the tall and striking Nahed from Palestine and the delightful Shereen from Egypt. I could always tell when they were on the Men's Campus because the library was busier. I know because I helped make it so, even though nearly all the reading material was in Arabic.

"I just read the magazines for the pictures."

Sometimes, I'd see Ghada, Nahed, and Shereen on the party circuit. Their presence surprised me at first, but it didn't take long for me to figure out such get-togethers were mainly manufactured opportunities for the sexes to mix in proper company. Under the guise, partygoers could engage in "reconnaissance work" because in the conservative Gulf country, surely nothing improper could occur with so many prying eyes. Surely.

There were also nights out at the pubs and discos in the Hilton and InterContinental Hotels, if only to see some women. Mostly, it was just colleagues from the Women's Campus, the waitresses, maybe a nurse or secondary school teacher, and the occasional belly or Russian dancer. You'd think there would've been some, some female tourists. You'd think, but tourism was not yet a thing back then. It's why most outside the Gulf had not yet heard of Dubai and Abu Dhabi, much less the sleepy desert oasis of Al Ain.

I was partly to blame that men so outnumbered women in the UAE, my presence contributing to the disparity that made the country the most "man-heavy" in the world. Why a few of us jokingly referred to the United Arab Emirates as The World's Largest Men's Club. In 1990, the year before my arrival, statistics say there were 191 males in the UAE for every 100 females - approximately 2 out of every 3 residents men. In 2010, three years after I departed, that ratio was 292 to 100 - approximately 3 out of every 4 residents men. While the disparity was even greater than when I arrived, that year, the UAE lost its status as The World's Largest Men's Club to another rapidly developing Gulf country, Qatar, sporting 314 males for every 100 females.

But for all the years I lived in the UAE, in no other country were women so outnumbered, and too many of those that were there were shuttered away. And even when I saw a woman, often there wasn't much to see, many covered in black from head to toe. Why, after only a few months, I figured I'd already been in the UAE too long when I caught myself gazing at a woman, the little voice inside my head saying, "Whoa... check out the ankles on that one."

047

IN PERSON

"How do I mail you a birthday card in Ecuador?"

"You don't, Grandma."

"Why not?"

"Because I don't have a mailing address."

Even though I never had a proper street address in the United Arab Emirates, I always had a mailing address - that of my employer, my address the same as everyone I worked with, a box number. My only address, it was sometimes a problem as many businesses wouldn't deliver to a box, to the UAE, or both.

Thankfully, Land's End did because I detested shopping for clothes, especially when I could order from a catalog and have them delivered to Ma's door, or my office mailbox in the UAE. Why virtually all my work shirts, pants, and neckties had a Land's End tag sewn into them. Based in Dodgeville, Wisconsin, not far from Platteville, I was buying local, at a distance, and every time a box from Land's End arrived, it was like getting a care package from home because it was.

If only every business had the same attitude as Land's End, or my Grandma Curran, because as long as she could send me a birthday card, as she'd always done when she couldn't deliver it in person, she didn't care if my address was a box number.   Others did, though, banks in particular a problem to deal with, as new regulations required them to verify the identity of every customer.   It's why the process for opening an account at a bank in Jersey, the largest of the Channel Islands between England and France, was, for me, more complicated than usual.

Even though I already had an account at the bank's Dubai branch, the Jersey branch still wanted to verify that I was who I said I was. The telephone conversation went something like this…

"Mister Curran, what is your mailing address in the UAE?"

"Box…"

"Sorry, sir, but box numbers are not allowed.   What is your street address?"

"I don't have one."

Silence… "Where do you live?"

"In an apartment building."

"It doesn't have an address?"

"No."

"How do you find it?"

"I know where I live."

"Then how do others find it?"

"I give good directions."

Silence…   "What about your electric bill?   Does that have an address?"

"Yes."

"What is it?"

"Box…"

"Sir, I cannot open an account for you without a proper mailing address."

"But everyone in the UAE has a box number for a mailing address. Call your branch in Dubai. Ask them what their address is. It's Box…"

It took some doing, but the Jersey branch opened an account for me, relying on the word of their Dubai branch that I was who I said I was - a teacher, not a terrorist or money launderer. And that I was a resident of the UAE, a country where the President once owned what *TIME* magazine described, on its cover no less, as "The World's Sleaziest Bank."

To open an account at the Dubai branch, I'd already gone through the whole rigmarole, presenting them with my passport, residency visa, and a reference letter from my employer. The difference? They knew all mailing addresses in the UAE were box numbers, including theirs, so it was a relatively painless process.

After moving to Ecuador, I no longer had a mailing address - Vilcabamba not a part of the country's limited mail service. By then, though, there were so many more efficient ways to communicate that no one cared, except for my then 86-year-old Grandma Curran. What she knew was going to the five-and-dime, buying a card, signing it, including a handwritten note, stuffing it all into an envelope, addressing the envelope, affixing a stamp, putting it in her mailbox, and then flipping up the flag, that "technology" now blocked, and she never used a computer.

After we moved to Ecuador, we discovered neither had nearly all our neighbors, no matter their age. Word-of-mouth was the most popular technology to pass along information between neighbors who'd been neighbors for who knows how many generations. Two old-school bulletin boards, one mounted on an exterior wall at the school in Chaupi and the other on the wall outside the monastery just up the road from our house, dispersed information from the outside world.

That the bulletin boards were often empty testified to how little the outside world intruded on the valley.

The only regular notice was the monthly one for when residents could pay their electric bills. Then, a pair of shoes often the only form of transportation for most of our neighbors, the power company sent a representative to the school in Chaupi, where residents could settle their accounts.

The school had two buildings (one classroom each), a basketball/soccer court, a volleyball court, and a four-holer outhouse. Other than a handful of houses and a small grocery store that a woman ran out of hers, that's about all there was to fabulous downtown Chaupi.

So small, I could throw a stone from one end of town to another. So small a shout could be heard all over town and in the "suburbs." So small, "Welcome To" and "Come Again" could appear on the same sign, in Spanish, of course. In Wisconsin, many a wide spot in the road has three taverns and a gas station, but our humble barrio didn't have any of those things, including the necessary four corners.

The officious but friendly woman from San Pedro, the nearest town, arrived via taxi with her printouts, a receipt book, and a small bag of change for the cash transactions. Early days, I made the five-minute walk to the school to pay because Sue didn't know any Spanish. Once she learned enough, she made the walk, I joining her every now and then to let the neighbors know we were still a couple, we otherwise low-profile people.

The last time I went, a neighbor boy from around the bend and up the hill followed me down the road, the power company not caring how old a payer was, only that someone paid. Ahead of me was Manuel, the father of the family that lived next to and across the road from us. Paying his and his adult children's bills, my wait in the queue was even longer. Even though his family had lived there for... ever, when it came

Manuel's turn to pay, the woman always asked for his and his children's names, but when it was my turn, she always knew my name without asking.

Did I stand out in a crowd? Yes, as the only gringo who paid in person, I was also a head taller than many of our neighbors, the disparity in height highlighted as I awaited my turn in a classroom chair, my knees near my ears, the furniture built for kindergartners, Ecuadorian kindergartners. While waiting, I often took the opportunity to engage my neighbors in conversation, giving me a chance to practice my Spanish and they a chance to laugh at my Spanish.

The process could last an hour, but there were few places better to wait, the setting gorgeous. I doubt I would've learned much in the Chaupi school because I would've spent my time staring out the window - looking at the clouds, the mountains, the trees, the birds, the bees, the bugs, the flowers, along with the chickens, geese, goats, burros, horses, cows, and people ambling by.

When it was my turn to pay, I wished the woman would've whispered the amount so the others couldn't hear - our monthly electric bill $25 to $30. Our neighbors didn't need the reminder that we had more money, as their bills were often no more than $5, sometimes less than $2, mainly because they owned few things with electrical cords. Why I was delighted to learn the chatter one Saturday morning was over another gringo, who lived in the high-end gated community just beyond Chaupi, and his electric bills, over $10,000 per month. $10,000! Just like that, we all felt poor.

He didn't pay in person, of course, not for a bill that large. As it was possible to pay at one of the power company's offices, many gringos did just that. Even Sue stopped going to the school to pay the electric bill when she learned it had become possible to pay at what passed for a bank in town, saving her a trip to the Chaupi school each month.

Now, I told you all that to tell you about another telephone conversation I had with another bank employee, this one in the States. I wanted to open an account there a few years after we moved to Ecuador. Of course, the bank representative wished to verify my identity. I did what I could, providing them with copies of my passport, residency visa, property deed, and property tax bill. I even sent a map showing a view of our property from space.

The bank eventually opened an account for me, which was surprising, considering our telephone conversation went something like this…

"Mister Curran, what is your mailing address in Ecuador?"

"I don't have one."

Silence… "No address?"

"There's no mail service here, so…"

"What is your street address then?"

"I don't have one."

Silence… "No address?"

"No, no one here has one."

"OK… then could you send me a copy of your electric bill?"

"Sure, but it doesn't have an address either."

"Why not?"

"As I said, we don't have one."

"Then how does the power company bill you?"

"They don't."

"Then how do you pay your bill?"

"In person."

048

A Second Second chance

I shanked it. I had a chance to kick a last-second field goal for the win, but I shanked it. I didn't keep my head down. I didn't keep my eye on the ball. Instead, I looked up to see what a kicker usually sees when they look up too soon - the football not splitting the uprights. With my miss, the score remained tied at 14 in a game we would lose in overtime. I let my team down, I let myself down, and I disappointed at least a couple-two-three dozen fans in the stands for what was just a high school junior varsity football game. That fact did not make me feel any better.

As a kicker (and a punter), I didn't get to play much. There was a lot of standing around between kicks, but when it was my time, I stood alone. Everyone could see just how well I did my job or didn't. If a lineman missed a block, many fans wouldn't notice, but if I shanked a kick, everyone saw - there nowhere to hide. Moreover, there was no guarantee I'd get a shot at redemption.

Unlike other position players who could come back and do what they did the next play, as a kicker, opportunities to make or miss a last-second kick don't come around as often as you might think. Amazingly, some kickers make it to the professional ranks without ever having had the opportunity to make or miss a game-winning field goal. I already had one, in high school... and I shanked it. I vowed to keep my head down if I ever got a second chance. I'd keep my eye on the ball. I'd make that kick.

My second chance came the following season, on September 26, 1980. Once again, the score was tied at 14, and just nine seconds remained on the clock when Coach Mohr called timeout and then called for the field goal team. As I made my way onto the field, Coach yelled, "C'mon Johnny!" slapping my helmet so hard I was grateful I had the remainder of the timeout to recover from the hardest hit I would take that night.

The score reflected the closely contested game. Usually, we handled the Winneconne Wolves with ease, but that night, they were hanging with us, having tied the score with a touchdown and a two-point conversion late in the first half. The defenses then dominated until we got the ball at our own 22 with 4:55 remaining in the game.

As I entered the huddle, I saw ten teammates who were pretty juiced, if not nervous. Attempting to break the tension, I asked, "You guys want to play overtime?" Tired, dirty, sweat-soaked faces that had just marched the ball almost all the way down the field told me, "No," they did not. "OK, then, let's do it."

If a last-second kick decides a game, the kicker usually gets the credit for the win, but kickers don't win games because they need their teammates to provide them with the opportunity to do so. That night, Ross's passing, Jeff's running, the line's blocking, and Tom's everything gave me that chance. In fact, it was Tom's incredible diving sideline snare on the game's final drive that told me I'd better get my leg loose.

Tom was also my holder and the best holder I ever had. Even when I was kicking at the football factory known as the University of Florida, I never saw anyone who could compare. Tom was that good at what was an important but thankless job. Thankless because the only time anyone ever hears about a holder is when he botches a snap, but with his sure hands, Tom never did that. He always placed the ball right where I wanted it, just the way I wanted it. He was a major part of my success.

Tom was also a good kicker, so good I have no doubt he would've been the team's kicker if not for me. No worries, he got plenty of playing time, earning the football team's Most Valuable Player award... and the basketball team's... and the baseball team's... even though he stood just five-feet-four inches and weighed 140 pounds. Bomber had talent... and heart.

While my miss the previous year had come in a junior varsity game, this time, my opportunity for a game-winning kick came in a varsity game, Friday night, under the lights at Waupaca's Haberkorn Field. The stands were packed on both sides that pleasant autumn evening, and even more fans lined the fence inside the running track encircling the field.

In Waupaca, everyone knew everyone or knew someone who did. So even if their kid wasn't playing, someone's was, or was a cheerleader, in the pep band, working the concession stand, or just a fan at the game in need of some adult supervision from a discreet distance. In Waupaca, Friday night football was a social event, but no invitation was needed, just a ticket.

There were the regulars, the neither snow nor rain nor heat nor gloom of night win or lose fans. Vi was there. Tom's mother, she went to every game everywhere. I remember how happy I was when she won a most deserved Fan of the Year award. Just one more piece of hardware in the family's trophy case, next to all the awards her son won.

Wayne and Barb were there. They, too, won a Fan of the Year award. Seeing their friendly faces at road games made even a place like Hortonville feel less hostile. Wayne was a big guy with curly hair and a beard and usually stood on the track next to the fence in his Friday night "uniform" consisting of work boots, blue jeans, and a buffalo plaid flannel shirt under his tan insulated vest. One of my biggest fans, I often chatted with Wayne while we watched the game during my downtime between kicks.

Another fan of mine, Bud, lived across the road from me. I was always out kicking the football around our yard, in the snow, rain, or heat, and sometimes even in the gloom of night. One afternoon, I was using a utility pole as a target for my kicks as Bud watched from his front stoop. I didn't mind an audience as it added some pressure to my practice.

After a particularly good day of hitting the pole, fortunately not good enough to knock out power to the neighborhood, Bud came over. After an exchange of pleasantries, he told me, "You can really kick that ball, John. Just keep at it. Your leg will take you places." Obviously, I still remember his much-appreciated words of encouragement.

But of all the people who attended the games, my best friend since the third grade, Dan, did not, or more accurately, could not. By the time I was playing on Friday nights, he was already chief cook and bottle washer at the Oakwood Villa, then Waupaca's largest restaurant and banquet hall. Despite the fact he was only 17 years old, the Chicken Man was perhaps Oakwood's most indispensable employee, so getting a

Friday night off was a rarity, but that Friday night, he did. It would be the only time Dan ever saw me play.

Also in the stands that night was Brenda - yes, that Brenda - the pretty girl who, just the Friday before, asked me to be her escort on the Homecoming Court. Even though her invite still hadn't sunk in, I was well aware another pair of eyes would be watching me - no pressure! I didn't want to disappoint her or do anything to make her regret her invitation.

Ma and Del were in the stands, of course. Del was easy to spot as he wore my bright orange University of Florida Fighting Gators baseball cap. A cap I purchased at an Eau Claire department store as a reward after Florida Head Coach Charley Pell invited me to join the Gators football team as a walk-on the following year. I wore that cap everywhere except that Friday night when it topped Del's head.

It seemed everyone was there - Yoko may have even brought her walrus. And when everyone looked at the scoreboard, they all saw Home 14, Visitor 14, and nine seconds on the clock. At the north end of Haberkorn Field, the football rested on the 10-yard line, left hash mark, as everyone on the field took their places. As always, there was that eerie calm, on the field anyway, just before the ball was snapped and the opposing lines exploded in head-banging fury - one side trying to block the kick, the other trying to prevent that.

Seven yards south of the ball was Tom, down on one knee. I was a further two steps south and one to the west. When I was ready, I gave Tom a nod. He turned, waiting to receive the snap from Dave…

Head down… Eye on the ball…

For all the buildup, it was over in an instant. The snap and hold were perfect, and when I finally looked up, the kick was perfect.

"GOOD!"

Jubilation!

Celebration!

Realization… that a penalty flag was lying on the field, Colbert, the right end, had jumped offside. That was a five-yard penalty, and my kick, my second chance, would not count. There were now only six seconds on the clock. It's a good thing Coach called timeout when he did because if he'd waited six seconds longer, time would have expired during my first kick, and I… I would not have gotten a second second chance.

With the football now resting on the 15-yard line, left hash mark, once again everyone on the field took their places, including Tom and I, now five yards further south than we were before. Tom's spot was 32 yards from the goalposts provided by the Waupaca Foundry, the town's largest employer. When I was ready, I gave Tom a nod. He turned, waiting to receive the snap from Dave…

Head down…

Eye on the ball…

Looking to the home side stands after the kick, there was Ma and Del, in a sea of happy Waupaca Comets football fans, Del waving my Florida Gators hat. He was so proud. So was Ma. I know if I'd missed that kick, I couldn't have looked, no way, no how. With everything that had happened - Brenda's invite, Dan finally getting to see me play, a game-winning kick, a town full of happy football fans - life was about as good as it got.

I was fortunate to get a second chance and then a second second chance because too many never get a first. At some later date, when I reflected on my experience with last-second kicks, I decided the penalty on Colbert was karma, karma that required me to make a second kick for shanking the one in the JV game the previous year. To this day, I wonder if I would've made that second chance kick, and then the second second chance kick, if I'd not shanked the earlier one, because I learned far more from that miss than from any kick I attempted.

The local newspaper, the *Waupaca County Post*, published just once a week, wouldn't come out until Thursday. I'd be headline news in the sports section, "Comets Kick Wolves With Curran and Character." In the photo accompanying the write-up, Tom and I both had our arms up, signaling the kick was good - Tom's directed at Coach, mine toward the newspaper's photographer - seemed about right.

Undoubtedly one of my happiest and proudest moments, that game-winning kick never had a chance to go to my head, though, because the day before I could read all about it, life reminded me it was only a football game. For on that following Wednesday, Bud suddenly and unexpectedly lost his wife. His three children lost their mother. Betty was just 35 years old.

From the moment I was old enough to listen, Ma'd been telling me, "Life isn't fair." Enjoying one of the best times of my life, I only needed to look across the road to know what she'd always told me… was true.

049

AMPUTATE!

Somehow, I managed 11 years before requiring my first and so far only trip to a hospital emergency room. I only had myself to blame, sustaining a nasty gash just below my right knee courtesy of some aluminum siding attached to the house I crashed into.

"Who leaves their house in the middle of a yard?"

Some might disagree, but I'm usually more careful. Want proof? That was the only knee-on collision I ever had with a house. That's what I got for wearing shorts instead of pants on a hot summer night in Albert Lea, Minnesota, visiting my cousins and their parents, my Aunt Judy and Uncle Gary.

The knee-on collision occurred during a rousing game of kick-the-can with my just older cousin Steve and some other kids in the neighborhood. Despite my injury, I kept playing because I was a boy, I was 11, having fun, and the cut didn't seem so bad, to me anyway. But when Steve saw my leg, by then covered in blood, he thought it serious enough that I should go inside to show his mother.

In retrospect, Steve's "concern" was probably less about my health and more about wanting to freak out his mother. Nevertheless, with blood streaming down my right shin, I made my way inside the back door of his house, where the first person I encountered was not my Aunt Judy but my cousin Lisa, standing at the kitchen sink washing the dinner dishes.

"Lisa, where's your mother?"

"Why?"

"Lisa, where's your mother?

"Why?"

I could see this was getting me nowhere, so I held out my blood-covered leg so Lisa could see why.

"MOM! JOHN'S BLEEDING ALL OVER THE KITCHEN FLOOR!"

To Lisa, I'm sure my bloody leg looked far worse than it was, but when her mother saw my bloody leg, Judy grabbed her car keys and hustled me out the door. During the drive to the hospital, she was relatively calm, but then she had four kids, so it probably wasn't her first trip to an emergency room. It probably wasn't her last, either.

At the hospital's emergency room entrance, we walked through the first of two sets of sliding glass doors only to find that the second set wouldn't open. That's when Aunt Judy's relative calm turned to frantic panic after the first set of doors closed behind us and wouldn't open, leaving us stuck in the middle. Her pounding on the inner doors while screaming for help did not bring any.

Looking around the vestibule for an alternate solution to our situation, I spotted and then pointed out a white wall-mounted rotary telephone, the same color as the wall, not easily seen under duress. When Aunt Judy saw it, she lunged for it, still screaming into the mouthpiece when hospital staff finally poured through the doors, probably expecting to find a kid missing at least a leg.

As blood continued trickling down my leg, a man already in his jammies at 8 pm took me to an exam room... for interrogation.

"What's your name?"

"John."

"How old are you, John."

"11, almost 12."

"Was that woman who brought you in your mother?"

"No, that was my Aunt Judy?"

"Do you live in Albert Lea?"

"No, I live in Wisconsin."

"How did you cut your knee?"

"I crashed into a house."

"You crashed into a house?"

"I wasn't watching where I was running."

"I see. So what cut your leg?"

"Aluminum siding."

By the time he finished questioning me, my cut had stopped bleeding on its own, the angry red gash then easy to see. With tweezers, he picked out bits of grass floating in the wound. Once he'd prepped my leg, almost a doctor left the room and left me alone.

A few anxious minutes later, two doctors wearing white coats entered. On the opposite wall, they jammed an X-ray into the top of a light box and flipped on the switch. Even from across the room, I could tell it was an X-ray of a lower leg. After carefully examining the ghostly image, the two nodded in agreement.

"We'll have to amputate."

"AMPUTATE! IT'S NOT THAT BAD!"

"No, no, sorry, son. Not you."

"OK then."

Only after accepting their apology did I realize no one had taken an X-ray of my knee.

A few minutes later, another doctor who would sew up my cut with four stitches entered the room. As I sat and watched, hunched over as far as I could to get a better look, I couldn't help but notice how the whole operation resembled Grandma Wall repairing a tear in the knee of my jeans. Except my leg wasn't made of cotton, and she didn't give my jeans an injection first.

"In a couple of weeks, make an appointment with your doctor, and they'll remove your stitches."

"OK."

When it was time to leave, Aunt Judy and I exited the hospital out the front doors, not the emergency doors.

After two weeks, my stitches had healed as hoped - the skin had closed up, a scar had formed, the whole area turning dry, crusty, and itchy in a healthy sort of way. Ma was about to make an appointment to have my stitches removed until she took a look at my knee.

"What happened to your stitches?"

"I pulled them out."

The day before, I'd noticed a loose thread. So I pulled on it, pulling my stitches like I'd seen Grandma do with fabric. The feeling of the thread sliding through my itchy skin was strangely pleasant, making me wish I could've pulled it through again... and again... and again...

050

WHERE DID YOU GET THIS VISA?

"Sorry, John. I can't do it."

"Huh?"

"Sorry, I can't do it. It's against Wisconsin law."

"What?"

"I'm not allowed to authenticate such documents. It's a violation of state statutes."

The government of the United Arab Emirates wanted to know whom they were hiring, especially since the Gulf War had just ended and security was tight. Before I could begin work at UAE University in Al Ain, not only did my credentials have to be verified, but I also had to be verified.

Paperwork can be intimidating, even more so if it's government paperwork. And with that paperwork for the United Arab Emirates government, it was even more daunting. Fortunately, most of what I needed to complete was in English, even though the visa I would get in return for my efforts would be in Arabic.

Despite being the major tourist destination the UAE has since become, tourism was all but illegal back then. You were not welcome unless you were an Emirati, other Gulf citizen, or a UAE-sponsored worker. The expense and rigamarole required to get Ma a visa to visit me in 1993 was its own story, just not this one.

Each of the documents required of me had to be authenticated. In most circumstances, that would mean a trip to a notary public, but these were not normal circumstances. For me, the notary was but the first hurdle in the steeplechase that was getting my first UAE visa. After the notary, I was then required to have my documents authenticated by my county of residence (Waupaca), my state of residence (Wisconsin), and my country of residence (USA) before I could submit them to the UAE Embassy in Washington, D.C. for final approval.

Even getting my documents notarized proved unexpectedly problematic when Gus, a Waupaca realtor, questioned the authenticity of my transcripts from the University of Wisconsin-Milwaukee.

"How do I know these are your official transcripts, John?"

"Really, Gus? How many times have I piloted you around the Chain on the Chief?"

While Gus was only giving me the business, he had a point. How did he know my transcripts from UWM really were my transcripts? Sure, they had their own stamp, seal, and signature verifying their authenticity, but Gus wondered if forgery was just another of my skills, along with piloting the Chief.

"...and all these A grades... seems a bit... suspicious."

But Gus eventually notarized my documents, giving his seal of approval to my student transcripts, birth certificate copy, passport copy, police report (ensuring I was not a criminal), health certificate (ensuring I wasn't about to die), and driver's license copy. No doubt grateful for the Emirati government's bureaucracy, he happily received payment for each notarized document.

"Enjoy your new boat, Gus!"

Despite his questioning of just how he could be sure the documents he was notarizing were the real deal, Gus' seal of approval was really the only one that mattered. Based on his authority, the other government levels merely rubber-stamped his declaration as to the authenticity of my documents. I think.

Except one. Located on Waupaca's east side, I'd never been inside the newly constructed Waupaca County Courthouse. I've only been inside once since, to visit Julie, a former classmate who worked in the Veterans Service Office. I'd parked in the adjacent lot numerous times, walking over to Haberkorn Field for a Waupaca High School football game, but every time I parked there, I remembered the first time I was inside.

Mary, the Waupaca County Clerk, and I had crossed paths before as she almost always attended an annual fundraiser on the Chief Waupaca. I was always the captain for the three-hour evening charter of glad-handing, speechmaking, dining, and raffle drawing, but when I approached the counter, she had no idea who I was until I introduced myself. Now, if I'd been wearing my captain's hat…

"Oh, John, yes, how can I help you today?"

I explained to Mary that the UAE government had just hired me to teach at their national university in the oasis city of Al Ain.

"Congratulations! The UAE? Where's that?"

"Conveniently located between Saudi Arabia and Iran."

"Ah, I see. So what do you need from me?"

I showed her the list of government authorities I needed to authenticate my documents.

"Gus already notarized them. Next on the list is you, the County Clerk."

So when Mary told me she couldn't, that doing so would violate Wisconsin law, at that moment, I understood the expression "hitting the wall" far better than I wanted to, or even expected to. Here I was, attempting to clear an early hurdle, in my hometown no less, and already what the UAE required of me could not be done.

Sensing my dismay and also my disbelief, Mary invited me behind the counter, where she showed me a shelf full of thick books. Pulling one down, she opened it to the page stating that what I asked her to do was prohibited. There it was. In black and white. How could I argue with a book written, printed, and distributed by the government?

"Sorry, John, but I can't do what you ask."

Standing in stunned silence, I thought, "What now?" when Mary offered, "How about I give you a document stating, as County Clerk, I cannot do what they ask?"

"Yeah, that just might work!"

Mary took my instruction sheet and sat at her desk, typing up a document stating she could not authenticate the documents as requested, citing the Wisconsin state statute forbidding it. After she pulled the document from her IBM Selectric (ask an older person), she signed, stamped, and sealed it before handing it to me for my approval.

"This is great, Mary! Thanks!" While it was, the document, with so little text, seemed… lacking.

"Mary, could you please do me one more favor?"

"What's that?"

"Could you add a few more stamps, seals, and signatures? I don't think it matters if they're relevant or not. It's just that others have told me when presenting paperwork to the Emirati government, the more stamps, seals, and signatures, the better."

"Sure!" So, with the aid of her assistant, they added more pomp and circumstance to the impromptu document.

"Could you please put some seals on the back of the document too?"

"Sure!"

"Thank you, Mary!"

It must've been enough because not only did the Secretary of State of Wisconsin authenticate my documents, but so did the Secretary of State of the United States. And, of course, the staff at the UAE Embassy in Washington, D.C. must've been sufficiently satisfied to affix a visa to my passport and mail it back to me, arriving only days before my scheduled departure.

The waiting was the hardest part because, given the number of hurdles to clear and the time constraint, whether or not I would get the visa in time was always going to be close. If not for stepbrother Jay, who was working at the Pentagon, I wouldn't have gotten the visa in time because he picked up my documents from the U.S. State Department, hand-delivered them to the UAE Embassy, then prodded the staff to expedite my paperwork given my fast approaching departure date.

If I had to wait for the State Department to send my documents back to me and then send them to the UAE Embassy, my departure date would've surely come and gone without a visa. I might've been out of a job, but at least I wouldn't have been out the money for a one-way ticket to Abu Dhabi, the Emirati government having already paid British Airways for that. But without a valid UAE visa in my passport, British

Airways agents would've prevented me from boarding my flight from Chicago's O'Hare Airport to London's Heathrow. Otherwise, British Airways would've had to pay for my return trip.

I think the paperwork process was the Emirati government's way of auditioning potential employees to determine whether or not they could survive working in a country that often frustrates foreigners like me. During my time in the UAE, I witnessed expats, even Arabic speakers, reduced to tears, so utterly frustrated by the bureaucracy. I figured the UAE government wanted to see if I could do the near impossible because if I couldn't, I had no hope of lasting in the Emirates. Last, I did, though, living and working in the UAE for almost 15 years, acquiring three more visas to do so.

Make that four because, after all that, the Emirati government made that first visa obsolete in the week or so between when it arrived in the mail and when I attempted to use it. Why it took me an hour to get through immigration after I arrived in Abu Dhabi. While the man in charge of immigration that night finally permitted my entry, one of the first things I was required to do after I arrived in the UAE was complete the necessary paperwork... for another visa. At least I had my documents authenticated. Even so, it still took another month.

051

GORILLA.BAS

"GET OUT!"

"But…"

"GET OUT! NOW!"

I'd warned Ahmed about playing computer games in my classroom. In addition to the obvious reasons, most of the computer games purchased in the United Arab Emirates contained viruses, no extra charge, ones soon installed on student workstations. When a computer became inoperable, the student would move on, infecting yet another.

As a result, there were days I was fortunate to have half the computers in any classroom functioning, - the rest knocked out of service by viruses. Teaching was difficult enough on the Men's Campus at UAEU, with the limited interest in attending, much less learning, displayed by more than a few students. I didn't need them making my job harder by knocking out workstations playing silly games.

A favorite was *Gorilla*, an "artillery" game featuring two dueling apes lobbing explosive bananas at each other over a city skyline. Players would enter values for angle and velocity to determine the trajectory of the thrown bananas. The goal was to bomb the opponent's gorilla off their building or inflict enough damage to cause the building under the gorilla to collapse.

Coded in BASIC, copies were available in Dubai for 10 Dirhams ($2.70) on a 3.5-inch floppy disk (ask an old person) or a 5.25-inch floppy disk (ask an even older person). Of course, they were pirated, as were almost all software, music, and movies sold in the UAE, in the early 1990s anyway.

VHS tapes (ask an old person) were often of poor quality, but with the (still censored) Internet years away, almost no English language TV, and no English language movies screened in local cinemas, many of my English-only speaking colleagues were desperate enough to rent, or even buy them. I never did, instead smuggling in (uncensored) movies on 8mm videotapes. For TV, I had Ma record and send 10-hour VHS tapes of my favorite American TV shows and Green Bay Packers football games. Censors watched them first, and then I did.

Audio cassettes (ask an old person) were just 10 Dirhams each, and if I bought ten, I got an eleventh free, along with a handy vinyl carrying case. I bought hundreds of these, adding to my music collection and filling in gaps - songs I was missing primarily due to greedy record companies. These pirated cassettes even had a brand name - Thomsun Original. The Oxford English Dictionary had its definition of original. Thomsun had theirs.

Despite my frustration with infected computer workstations, I, too, had fun with *Gorilla*, although not in the same way as the students, thanks to a software program faculty had at their disposal called Broadcast. From any workstation, the classroom management software allowed me to see what each student was doing on their computer and even take control of it.

If I discovered a student playing *Gorilla*, sometimes, just for fun, I'd hijack their computer. Only for a few seconds, though, long enough to change the code in the student's copy of the game so no matter what values they entered for angle and velocity, the banana would fly off the screen (Angle: 45, Velocity: 999999999), never to return to the *Gorilla* cityscape. Game Over. The bewildered look on the student's face? Priceless.

If I felt particularly fiendish, I'd change the code so no matter what values the student entered, the banana would go straight up, then straight down (Angle: 90, Velocity: 2), turning the game's gorillas into suicide bombers. Game Over. The bewildered look on the student's face? Priceless.

If you were wondering, most students never figured out how to lock their floppy disks (ask an old person), and I wasn't about to teach them.

Advantage, Mister John.

But that day, it was just Ahmed's bad luck that my catching him playing *Gorilla*, again, was my last straw. When he didn't get up and go as requested, I ejected his game disk and snapped it in half in his face. When he still didn't go, I picked up his belongings and threw them down the aisle and out the open door at the back of the classroom.

That got him out of his seat and heading for the door, me on his heels. We talked as we walked, but I wouldn't call it a conversation, Ahmed shouting in Arabic and me in English. After gathering his belongings in the hallway, he resumed his diatribe in Arabic as I blocked the door to prevent him from returning to class. I stood in silence, letting him have his say, but when he ran out of words, I leaned in until we were nose to nose and said, "So's your mother."

While I had no idea what Ahmed had said, I must've guessed correctly because he jumped backward into the hallway, his astonished face even redder with embarrassment than it had been in anger. He tried to speak, but while his mouth moved, no words came out, in Arabic or English, before he turned and scurried down the hall like the little cockroach he was. That was the last I ever saw of Ahmed.

When I turned around, my remaining students, having spun around in their seats to watch the show, looked every bit as astonished as Ahmed had been. My apparently fitting reply to his heated remarks no doubt convinced many, if not all of my students, that I knew Arabic. I didn't, but I wasn't about to correct them.

Advantage, Mister John.

052

THE FIRST TRANSATLANTIC FLIGHT

Our epic journey began, as so many do, on a rickety old school bus. With the University of Wisconsin-Milwaukee campus just 80 or so miles from Chicago's O'Hare Airport, we were puzzled as to why the driver stopped the wheels of the bus from going round and round just over 20 miles from our destination, but stop he did, at the Lake Forest Oasis Travel Plaza.

Sure, it sounds picturesque, but there was no lake, forest, or oasis, not the kind with palm trees swaying in a desert breeze. What there was was a Wendy's restaurant and a gas station because the Travel Plazas were commercial rest stops built over the top of toll highways crisscrossing the Chicago metro area.

"Doug, you getting something to eat?"

"No."

"You know where your next meal is coming from?"

"No."

"Then you might want to get something to eat."

And this was when American air carriers included a meal in the ticket price, but I wasn't taking any chances. Besides, airline food is always a crapshoot... After convincing my friend to join me at Wendy's, I downed a four-cornered cheeseburger, fries, and a chocolate shake. With the addition of two, maybe three days' worth of the recommended daily allowance of salt, fat, and calories, on top of the breakfast I ate before getting on the bus, I figured I was good to go… to England.

One of 30 architecture students enrolled in a field study program at Oxford University, the three weeks of summer school came with an option for a fourth week in Paris, which most signed up for, including me. Leading the program was Gil, one of the few architecture professors at UWM I liked. He was also fluent in French and had architect friends in Paris, all reasons why, in addition to the obvious, I opted for the extra week.

When we arrived at O'Hare's Northwest Airlines check-in counter, we discovered Gil's Milwaukee-based travel agent, the one who got us such a good deal, that included a school bus ride, had screwed up. I wasn't sure what the travel agent had done or not done, as I wasn't at the front of the line, but a classmate at the counter turned to tell us, and everyone else in the terminal, "OH, MAN! GIL IS GONNA BE SO PISSED!"

Not only would our group not be flying direct from O'Hare to London's Gatwick Airport, we wouldn't even be flying together. Instead, a third of us would fly to Minneapolis, another third to Detroit, and my third to Boston, where we would catch direct flights to Gatwick. Adding to the drama, Gil was already in London, where he'd be awaiting our arrival on a flight from Chicago hours before we'd instead arrive on flights from Minneapolis, Detroit, and Boston. In 1989, before cell phones and the Internet, we had no way of letting him know our itinerary had changed.

After the flight to Boston's Logan Airport, our third experienced no problems connecting to Gatwick. With the group scattered about the coach cabin, you might think my having an aisle seat on an exit row behind a galley for the seven-hour transatlantic flight would be a good thing, maybe a great thing. I did. At first...

While there was not a smoker in sight, I soon discovered my seat location was next to another section, unofficial, for parents with small children. Diaper bags, blankies, bottles, toys, pacifiers, poop, pee, snot, vomit... it was all there. Right there because one new father, seated across the aisle in the center section during takeoff, spent most of the flight standing before me so as not to block the large TV screen in front of his seat as he held his squalling baby.

I just realized I never thanked him for that.

Instead of getting some sleep, I got seven hours of "WAAAAAHHHHH!" because whatever daddy tried to quiet his baby, it didn't work. The squalling, like the flight, seemed never-ending. Why I developed a powerful urge to pound on the cockpit door and do some screaming of my own, "ARE WE THERE YET?"

Much as I despised flying smokers, I believed their actions more than justified my disgust with them and their filthy habit. But a crying baby? Nothing it ate or pooped would be solid for months. How could I loathe the little guy without feeling like a monster?

As for the parents, who managed to avoid eye contact with me for the duration of the flight, my attitude toward them fell somewhere between the smokers and their baby - an uncomfortable mix of loathing and sympathy. That seven hours spent in a virtual daycare center may have been when I decided fatherhood was not for me.

I just realized I never thanked them for that.

Not that I would get much sleep, what with a flight attendant using my right knee not once, not twice, but three times as a bumper to get her food and drinks cart started down the aisle, with nary an apology, my right knee bruised and bloodied as a result. She was about to bang my knee a fourth time when I did the *Hokey Pokey*, putting my right foot out, stopping her cart short. After pulling up my pant leg to show her the knee and the damage done, I shot her... a thousand-yard stare... as I stated, ever-so-sweetly, "I hope our pilot has better depth perception than you do."

Why, I'm sure, my before-landing breakfast came with a complimentary loogie. Why, before I'd completed my first transatlantic flight, I envied Charles "Lucky" Lindbergh doing it solo because somewhere south of Greenland, I thought the plane plunging into the ocean might not be the worst thing. Why, when the pilot announced we were making a final approach to Gatwick, I was relieved, as was the frazzled father, still holding his baby, who had finally fallen asleep.

Of course.

As the pilot made all those last little maneuvers, telling me the runway was not far away, that I still couldn't see the ground was... troubling. Fog. London. Go figure. On occasion, I piloted the Chief Waupaca in fog so thick I had to navigate from memory, but if I crashed, maybe someone would lose a dock or a boat. Of course, there was always the possibility that such a collision might cause one of my passengers to spill their beer. "OH, THE HUMANITY!"

But landing a jumbo jet? With hundreds of passengers? When you can't see past the hood ornament jets should have but don't? I knew commercial airliners had computer navigation systems and all that, but you can't tell me landing a 747 in the fog when you can't see the runway isn't just a wee bit stressful for the pilot. Land it smoothly he did, however.

I thanked him for that.

Ours was the first of the thirds to arrive at Gatwick. After clearing immigration and customs, Gil was still there, waiting for us, even though we were hours late and arrived on a different flight than he'd expected. Why Gil had questions...

"What happened?"

Ask your travel agent."

"Where's the rest of the group?"

"On a flight from Minneapolis…"

"@$%*@#^!"

"…and Detroit."

"%&^#&$@#!"

"They should be here soon."

"How soon?"

"Today?"

"%&$#@$*%!"

Gil taught us some new curse words that morning, a few in French.

Then there was the return trip…

053

DEL NEVER WORE A SEATBELT

On a beautiful autumn afternoon, the kind that made me happy to live in Wisconsin, Del and I washed and waxed his car. The wax would protect the paint from the weather the coming Wisconsin winter would bring, the kind that made me wish I lived somewhere else. However, just 24 hours after putting a hard shell shine on Del's Dodge, life would remind me that Turtle Wax offered only so much protection.

Painted black, Del's Royal Monaco looked like an unmarked police car. Even more so after Del's friends at the Eau Claire County Sheriff's Department presented him with a big badge decal, which he pasted in the back seat driver's side window, all but blotting out the view.

Then there was the CB radio Del had installed, complete with a giant antenna mounted on the narrow metal strip between the trunk lid and back window. At the height of the CB radio craze, romanticized in C. W. McCall's chart-topping song "Convoy," Del's CB was a toy he just had to have.

But the chatter on the radio gave him something to listen to as he made the 150-mile trips between Eau Claire and Waupaca, while the 10-20s on the whereabouts of Smokey probably helped him avoid a few speeding tickets, at least enough to pay for the radio.

And maybe a new driving cap because Del was from a generation of men who wore hats for fashion, not just to keep their heads warm or shaded. While Del's hat of choice was the driving cap, he'd place it on top of the dashboard, right in the center, right where an unmarked police car might have a blue flashing light for the driver to pop onto the roof when the situation warranted.

With Del's Dodge looking like an unmarked patrol car, the Eau Claire County Sheriff's Department might just as well have put him on their payroll as his car's appearance alone was enough to help deter speeders. Del delighted in telling of drivers pulling alongside to pass, then easing back, fearful of getting a speeding ticket after mistakenly, but understandably, connecting the dots.

The trips between Eau Claire and Waupaca were necessary because Del lived in Eau Claire, working as a news presenter and talk show host on WOKL 1050 Radio, while Ma and I lived in Waupaca after she got her first teaching job at the local high school. So from the day after Christmas in 1971, when they were married, until August of 1980, when Del retired and moved to Waupaca, we were a two-household family.

Del made most of the trips, usually driving over Friday afternoons after he finished work at one. Arriving about when Ma got home from work at four, we were a one-household family until Sunday afternoon when Del returned to Eau Claire. But on this particular Sunday, an hour and a half or so after Del had driven his freshly washed and waxed Dodge out of our driveway in Waupaca, the telephone rang.

"Who could that be?"

Ma and I wondered out loud because the only person who called on Sunday afternoons was Del after he arrived in Eau Claire, but he wasn't due for at least another hour and a half.

While I don't much care for telephones, I despised that one. It was pale pink. Pink! Long before there were smartphones, or even cell phones, every time that wall-mounted rotary rang, the sound of the bells reverberated in the cavity behind the thin wood paneling, making any call all the more intrusive. And with the cord connecting the handset and the base inexplicably no more than two feet long, the user had no privacy.

So when Ma answered the phone, it didn't take long before I learned what had happened. A drunk driver had turned left in front of Del on Highway 54 just east of Wisconsin Rapids, abruptly halting his journey westward. The drunk turned left so late that Del had no time to slam on the brakes before slamming into the left front corner of the drunk's car at 50mph. Even though the drunk was not wearing his seatbelt, he managed to walk away from the crash without a scratch. Naturally.

Del never wore a seatbelt. Never. Ever. But for some reason, that day, he did. Pre-airbag, that seat belt may have saved his life, at least that's what Del said, calling from the Wood County Sheriff's Department. An hour or so later, after Ma and I arrived there, we saw the drunk driver, still so inebriated he was barely able to keep himself seated on a hallway bench. A woman Ma and I assumed was his wife came to collect him, but a woman at the desk - this not her first experience with this man - told us it was the drunk's mother, his repeated drinking to excess no doubt making him look a generation older than he was.

The next person we encountered was an ambulance-chasing lawyer who wanted to know if we needed his services. "Ummm... no." The drunk was clearly at fault, and despite the severity of the crash, thanks to Del wearing his seat belt, he didn't require medical attention - he only bumping his knee on the dashboard and grazing his head on the sun visor. At six-foot-two, he didn't have a lot of wiggle room, even in his big, black Dodge, now freshly washed, waxed... and totaled.

We almost lost Del that day. Given his aversion to seat belts, we were fortunate not to. He couldn't explain why he happened to buckle up the only time he was ever involved in an accident driving between Eau Claire and Waupaca. Ma and I were relieved he did because if he hadn't she would've needed that lawyer.

Well... a lawyer.

054

SE VENDE

"Green truck? You want?"

"What?"

"Green truck. Loja. You want?"

"Chamico… What did you do?"

"I talk with them. They will sell."

"SUE!"

In the United Arab Emirates, Sue and I each owned Jeep Wranglers, purchased together from the dealer in Dubai off Airport Road. We were virtual strangers then, but something about the librarian in the market for a new Jeep, like me, caught my eye. But you already know that story, so here's another…

Sue and I loved our Jeeps, but we had to sell after seven years of puttering them around the UAE and occasionally Oman. While they would've been great vehicles at our new home off a dead-end dirt road near Vilcabamba, Ecuador's rules would not allow us to import even one. Just because you want to move to another country doesn't mean you can. The same goes for importing vehicles.

Our search for a new ride began almost immediately upon our arrival in Ecuador. However, we were in no particular hurry as we managed just fine with the local pickup truck taxis and intercity buses. Not having a vehicle was only a problem when we needed a late-night lift when most taxi drivers were asleep, during Carnival when most were drunk and not working, or during the rainy season when it was raining.

We weren't sure what we wanted after we moved here anyway. At first, we considered buying a new pickup truck from a dealer in Loja. We decided against it after seeing what our dead-end dirt (we aspired to gravel) road did to a neighbor's new $50,000 pickup. After just six months, it looked six years old, and we were looking at a low-end model, not a high-end one we saw prematurely aging.

Putting us off new for used, every time we went to Loja, on the bus, we browsed the city's many used car lots. We kicked the tires on a number of vehicles, primarily pickups and SUVs, even inquiring about a Caterpillar bulldozer... just because. Whenever we saw a vehicle we liked tooling around town, we'd turn to each other and ask, "¿Se vende? (For sale?)" It got to be a running gag, one Sue and I still repeat whenever we see something we want, wondering if it's for sale, even if we know it's not.

After changing our minds many times, we determined that a Toyota FJ40 LandCruiser would best serve our needs. Given the condition of our road, especially during the rainy season, or the dry season, an FJ40 seemed perfect given its reputation for rugged reliability. A reputation I learned was well deserved during my first few years living in Al Ain because my neighbor, Peter, and his wife, Sylvia, had an old FJ45, the pickup truck version of the FJ40.

I referred to it as "The Toyota From Hell" because no matter what Peter did to it on his many desert excursions - he earning his own wing in the Al Ain Museum after donating the many artifacts he unearthed - he just couldn't kill it. Awakened from a nap one afternoon by the sound of a five-pound hammer meeting metal, I discovered it was Peter, dressed in his day-off kurta pajama, "fine-tuning" his FJ.

I wanted that truck! One I could take a hammer to, and no one would notice... or care. Then Sue and I wanted that kind of truck, one we could use and abuse, living on the side of a mountain in Ecuador. Also, purchasing an iconic Toyota FJ40 would help make up for the pair of iconic Jeep Wranglers we had to leave behind. Built from 1960 to 1984 and imported from Japan or the States, the problem was there weren't many FJ40s in our area, and even fewer were for sale.

We put Chamico, an entrepreneur from town, on the case. He found a red one for sale in Malacatos, a small town just north of us. We took a look, but it had some issues, enough that we didn't even make an offer. Then he found another, white, in Loja, but the owner wanted more than we were willing to pay, especially with parts of the not yet rebuilt engine scattered about his shop floor.

Sue and I even found our own FJ40, gray and in good condition, other than a flat tire. Parked in a corner lot of a used car dealer in Loja, we thought we'd found our truck. We looked under the hood, and there was an engine, in one piece. We gave three of the tires a good kick, but with the fourth flat, we couldn't take the truck for a test drive.

No one on duty was willing or able to repair it, but the dealer promised to fix it by the next day if we wished to return. Believing it might be the FJ40 we'd been searching for, we told him we'd be back. The following morning, we were, with money in our pockets, but the tire was still flat when we arrived at the lot. The dealer instructed his flunky, nowhere to be found the day before, to fix it, which he did.

We still never got to take that Toyota for a test drive, as the dealer couldn't come up with the paperwork or even the keys to the LandCruiser. "For fuck's sake…" was all Sue had to say. No papers. No keys. No sale. Stolen? Maybe, but it was surely not a legitimate vehicle. Dejected we were not riding home in a "new" FJ40, once again we returned to Vilcabamba, on the bus.

Even though there was no rush, our search proved frustrating, with mostly ourselves to blame after narrowing our focus to a hard-to-find truck. But partly to blame were the two FJ40s we found - one silver, one green - that taunted us nearly every trip to Loja. Why? Because both were almost always parked along the bus route, and neither was for sale.

When we checked out the silver one parked on a city street, no doubt in front of the owner's home, it appeared in excellent condition. Sue wanted it so bad that she suggested, "We should put a "Se Vende" sign in the truck's window, then ring the (presumed owner's) doorbell, see what happens." After another month or two of not finding what we wanted, we might've given that strategy a go.

We spotted the green one parked in front of an eye-catching two-tone blue and white house off the highway near the Loja city limits. Every time we passed it, on the bus, we'd turn to each other and ask, "¿Se vende?" but it never was, no sign in the window anyway, and parked well off the road up a private drive, we couldn't even check it out as we'd done with the silver one.

We had a chance to one afternoon, however. Riding in Chamico's box truck after hiring him to bring our new washing machine back from a store in Loja, we again spotted the green LandCruiser parked in its usual spot. As always, Sue and I turned to each other and asked, "¿Se vende?" Sue and I almost launched through the windshield after Chamico slammed on the brakes.

"You want to buy?" Chamico asked, pointing to the green LandCruiser.

"Yes, we do!"

While Chamico was more than willing to inquire, we didn't want to get involved in another deal on a day when we'd purchased a major appliance, one we hoped was still in one piece in the back of the truck after the too sudden stop. It took some doing, but we finally convinced Chamico to proceed to Vilcabamba.

Days later, after just enough time had passed for us to forget about our near crash test dummy experience, we heard a honk outside our gate, a sign for all of our neighbors to listen in so they, too, would know what was happening. It was Chamico, this time driving his little white Datsun 1200 UTE. Popular in Ecuador, the 1200 UTE was Datsun's version of a Chevy El Camino.

Seems the next time Chamico went to Loja, he stopped at the two-tone house and inquired about the green FJ parked out front. After Sue joined me at the gate, Chamico explained that it wasn't for sale, but the owners were willing to sell it… for the right price. The right price, while maybe $500 high - perhaps Chamico's commission, fair enough - seemed fair enough, especially for a vehicle that wasn't for sale.

Through Chamico, we arranged to meet with the truck's owners at their home in Loja. A lovely older couple, they trusted us to take their LandCruiser for a test drive, perhaps because we left Chamico's Datsun as collateral. The FJ made a positive first impression, starting with Sue's first turn of the key. As she drove around Loja, Chamico riding shotgun, me on a jump seat in the back, we discovered the truck had some issues - for one, a wonky steering wheel.

It mostly worked fine, even though an owner in the States or Canada might've scrapped it years before, not knowing its worth. But older vehicles are popular in Ecuador because they don't require all the sophisticated computer electronics to repair - just a guy with hand tools who knows what they're doing, like Sue's mechanic in Vilcabamba, Wilmer.

In our best Spanish, Sue and I told the owners that we were satisfied with the truck and their asking price. We agreed to meet the next day to do the paperwork at their lawyer's office in Loja, which turned out to be the same lawyer we used to do the paperwork when we bought our property two years previous. We arrived on time, and by on time, I mean half an hour early to make sure we weren't late. The owners, accompanied by their daughter, were late, but not more than an hour, so they were still on time in Ecuador.

Then we had to wait some more because Mama wouldn't come inside. On the sidewalk outside the lawyer's office, in tears, she didn't want to sell "her baby." From what we translated the day before, Mama and Papa were the vehicle's only owners, the truck a few years older than their daughter. Difficult as the situation was, we understood Mama's reluctance, as we didn't want to sell our Jeeps after seven years, and Mama had the Toyota even before she had her now adult daughter.

As Sue and I anxiously waited in the lawyer's office, Papa and the daughter were out on the sidewalk with Mama, coaxing her to co-sign the bill of sale. Half an hour later, she finally did.

"Whew!"

Just over a year after we moved to Ecuador, we had a vehicle, a 1974 Toyota FJ40 LandCruiser, one Sue now needed to drive back to Vilcabamba. We weren't sure, but we thought the tires might have been the ones installed at the factory in Japan, with only ghost tread remaining. Still, she drove the truck for months before getting the tires replaced, along with the rims, so old and rusted in spots that inner tubes had been required. However, besides replacing the carburetor and the battery, the green FJ40 never got or needed more than irregular maintenance.

Almost immediately after we bought it, people stopped at our gate asking if the truck on the other side was for sale. "¿Se vende?" In town, hopeful buyers also accosted Sue, pleading with her to sell. But a perfect vehicle for us and my birthday present for her that year, it wasn't for sale at any price. Until years later, after we purchased a second FJ40, a shiny red 1979 model.

055

MY TIME AS A VOLUNTEER FIREMAN

"FIRE!"

Jay and I were home alone one night watching TV, not playing with matches, when the roar of fire engines, wailing sirens, and flashing lights turning the inside of our house into a disco had us leaping from the sofa. Hustling down the street, we hoped for a pyrotechnic display of epic proportions, with seemingly every fire truck in the city gathering at the Eau Claire Academy.

After Ma and I moved from Eau Claire to Waupaca in August 1971, the following summer, and just for that summer, Ma and Del rented a house for the four of us on Erin Street located in a residential neighborhood on Eau Claire's north side. The house was a block from the Academy, a treatment center for troubled youths, and where I was born when it was Sacred Heart Hospital.

But there would be no pyrotechnic display of epic proportions as firemen quickly extinguished the blaze. The hot spot was a dorm room mattress, the smoldering mass tossed from a third-floor window, landing in the parking lot below with a smoky flop. Much to our disappointment, that was as exciting as it got.

Jay was barely old enough to drive, but with press credentials from his deejay job at WOKL 1050 Radio, he asked the fire chief for the story. Seems a couple of Academy residents, apparently bored with watching Eau Claire's one and only TV station, decided to roast some marshmallows. Of course, you need a fire for that, and it got out of control. There were no injuries, although a small portion of the building suffered minor smoke damage.

Much ado about nothing compared to our first fire that summer because a few weeks previous, a gathering cloud of thick, black smoke, rapidly turning a sunny summer day into night, had Jay and I running down the hill - downtown Eau Claire really down, sitting in a bowl at the confluence of the Chippewa and Eau Claire Rivers. At the bottom of the Madison Street hill, Jay and I no longer needed the smoke to guide us because we could see and feel the fire at a Uniroyal tire warehouse, an old red brick building alongside the Chippewa River.

We later learned that some youths had broken into the warehouse. Apparently bored after finding nothing more than stacks of tires, they did something people did to entertain themselves years before there were smartphones - they whittled. They then got the bright idea to set their pile of wood shavings on fire, and it got out of control.

The raging tire fire, as seen from the A&W Root Beer stand two blocks away, as close as police permitted gawkers, was a spectacular sight for a boy a spit short of ten years old. But even from that distance, the intense heat and choking smoke extinguished any thoughts I may have had of ever becoming a fireman. Sliding down a pole, riding in a big red truck with flashing lights, a wailing siren, and a spotted dog sounded good until that day when I learned what the job was really about.

So, a decade later, my first year at the University of Wisconsin-Platteville, I was surprised when I joined a volunteer fire brigade. I don't remember why I joined. Like the youths at the Eau Claire Academy or in the Uniroyal tire warehouse, perhaps I was bored, Platteville the kind of place where students traveled 22 miles down the highway to Dubuque, Iowa, in search of a good time.

Consisting entirely of residents from the 4th Floor North Hugunin Hall dormitory on the UWP campus, it mattered not that our all-volunteer brigade was a ragtag bunch with no formal training because we were a dedicated firefighting unit. No matter what was on TV, if there was an exam to study for, tater tots on the menu at the campus cafeteria, or a rare female sighting on our floor, we responded when duty called.

Like all fire brigades, we had a fire chief, a young man named Paul. He was chief because he founded the brigade and had a fire chief hat. Made of red-molded plastic, it looked like almost any other fireman's hat, except for the combination of flashing red light and siren mounted on top. I know I was impressed with perhaps the best thing anyone ever purchased at Radio Shack.

Paul wasn't all hat, though, as the guy had a nose for fires, probably because he spent more time than anyone in the janitor's closet... looking after his fish. Paul kept the fish, live bait for his numerous fishing expeditions, in the closet's floor sink because the university did not permit aquariums in dorm rooms.

Lucky for us Paul spent as much time there as he did because it seemed like a fire broke out in the trash chute every other week. Across from the floor sink, the chute was where dorm residents disposed of their trash - pull the steel hopper door open, throw in the trash, and down the chute it went to a basement incinerator. Convenient, yes, although my roommate was just a tad too large to fit through the opening.

When Paul smelled smoke, he'd don his fire chief hat, activate the flashing red light and siren, and then take a lap around the squared O-shaped wing that was 4th Floor North in Hugunin Hall. The brigade would fall in behind Paul, forming a firefighting conga line of sorts. When all who were available were in tow, Paul would lead us to the janitor's closet.

Once inside, he'd open the door to the trash chute. One of the volunteer firefighters would then grab the hose from the janitor's floor sink and hand it to Paul, who would insert it into the chute. Once he signaled that the hose was secure, another volunteer opened the tap, the water shut off only after Paul signaled that the smoke had ceased.

"Well done, men!"

Paul then took roll call to ensure everyone was accounted for - we always were since he only called out the names of those present. We'd then return to our door rooms, each volunteer firefighter secure in the knowledge they helped extinguish yet another fire before it got out of control... and burned untold amounts of trash, the chute doubling as a chimney, the janitor incinerating what collected at the bottom every other week or so.

By the time the janitor noticed the incinerator fire was out and climbed the ten flights of stairs from the basement, our volunteer fire brigade had already returned to civilian life. I don't know why the janitor always suspected our wing was responsible. After all, there were three floors of suspects below us. Maybe it was due to Paul's live bait swimming in his fourth-floor floor sink.

"I know it's you guys! One day I'm going to catch you sonsofbitches!"

He never did.

I wonder if Paul, assuming he's now a father, ever told his kids about when he served as fire chief. If he did, you know those kids are proud of their pop.

056

MY GRANDPA WALL COULD FLY

It's happened to me... Maybe it's happened to you... In a hurry, you were driving along, and then you got stuck behind a car driven by an older man... wearing a hat. A hat you could barely see because his head barely rose above the back of his seat. He never signaled his intentions if he turned or changed lanes because "That's just what they'll be expecting me to do." While you were well aware of him, he seemed unaware of anything, including the fact that he was driving a car. And no matter how fast you were, were going, he was going at least 20mph slower.

If this ever happened to you, I can guarantee you were not stuck behind my Grandpa Wall. While he had a hat, he also had a lead foot, and a negative attitude toward any law enforcement officers inclined to give him a speeding ticket.

"They should be out catching real criminals!"

"Yes, Grandpa, we know..."

Grandpa had a point, why I found it interesting when I learned the United Arab Emirates had separate police forces for traffic and crime. Thing was, the UAE was virtually crime-free, easily the safest place I've ever lived, unless I got behind the wheel of my car, with or

106

without a hat, because driving in the UAE was far too often a breathtaking, heart-stopping experience. Mainly owing to speeders, or "overspeeders" in the local vernacular, especially those who blew by me... when I was doing 90mph.

"MANIAC! THIS IS A CITY STREET!"

Yet, no police officer ever issued me a speeding ticket because the UAE Traffic Police seemed indifferent to the high-speed demolition derby going on around them. Or perhaps they just didn't notice, crawling along on the side of the road at 10mph, sipping tea, reading a newspaper, at least one foot propped on the dashboard. There was a definite need for proactive policing, for which I was partly to blame.

Never, though, did I see anyone pulled over for speeding in my almost 15 years there. Why my Grandpa Wall would've loved driving in the UAE. He and most Emirati drivers also liked big cars with big engines, so he would've fit right in, even though his favorite makes were Dodge and Chrysler, while most locals preferred BMW and Mercedes.

Notorious for trading cars, the biggest, baddest car Grandpa ever wheeled and dealed for was a retired Wisconsin State Patrol cruiser. Black, with a 440 cubic inch engine and heavy-duty suspension, I was surprised he didn't keep it any longer than the few months he did, if for no other reason than revenge for the perceived and real harassment he received from law enforcement.

As a farm equipment salesman, Grandpa was often on the road. The police made his job that much more difficult by eagerly issuing speeding tickets.

"They should be out catching real criminals!"

"Yes, Grandpa, we know..."

If he deserved a ticket, Grandpa paid his fine, annoyed the police had nothing better to do when he knew they did. But if he honestly believed he didn't deserve a ticket, pity anyone involved because my Grandpa Wall, a man of principle unlike few I've ever known, would fight for what was right.

For example, the time he was driving a big old Chrysler through Dunn County, pulling a manure tank, and was given a speeding ticket. Grandpa returned to the scene of the crime and measured the distance from the STOP sign to where the police officer pulled him over. He also had his car and the manure tank weighed. Armed with this information, he used his knowledge of math and science to show that he could not have been going fast enough to warrant a speeding ticket in the distance traveled from a dead stop.

Aware of Grandpa's research, his friend, Carl, a state trooper, told the officer who cited Grandpa that he should probably skip court as he was doomed to lose. Grandpa beat the ticket and what turned out to be a corrupt system as the Dunn County judge was later exposed for receiving kickbacks on the fines resulting from drummed-up tickets. That dirty judge was exactly the kind of lawbreaker Grandpa thought the police should be hounding, not a hardworking family man like him trying to earn an honest buck... as fast as he could.

Then there was the time Grandpa went to jail for an overtime parking ticket, one he received in downtown Bloomer, just blocks from his home. He'd driven downtown to get a haircut, parking next to the city attorney's car in the municipal lot. After his haircut and the customary exchange of information with Kenny the barber, Grandpa returned to find the police had ticketed his car, but not the city attorney's. Grandpa refused to pay his fine. Weeks later, a Chippewa County Sheriff's Department officer served Grandpa with a summons to appear in court.

You might wonder why Bloomer's police chief would issue a summons over a simple parking ticket. Here's why. One night, Grandpa and Grandma were watching TV when they heard a loud noise on the street outside their house. When Grandpa went to investigate, he found his parked car demolished, another car having crashed into it. He called the police. The chief showed up with a patrolman. Realizing the culprit was drunk, and his cousin, the chief told the patrolman, "Take the driver home. He's having a heart attack."

Uh-huh.... The driver was never charged, and because he wasn't, Grandpa's insurance company was reluctant to make good on his totaled car. So Grandpa had a little chat with the chief about what course of action he would take if he didn't receive due compensation for his car. Grandpa got his money and a police chief with a grudge - who saw a chance for revenge by dragging Grandpa into court.

When Grandpa appeared in court, as ordered, the judge told him, "Three days in jail or a $25 fine."

"I'll go to jail."

"You can't pay?"

"Money isn't the problem. I received a parking ticket, but the city attorney didn't. I can't do anything about the corruption brought out by the Watergate scandal in Washington, but I can try to do something about corruption in my hometown."

Grandpa went to jail, where he had a good time playing cards with his fellow inmates.

"The food was pretty good too."

The story didn't end with Grandpa's release because his friend, state trooper Carl, you remember Carl, also served on the Bloomer city council. In the course of his duties, he'd seen the bills stemming from Grandpa's summons - court costs and the three days he spent in the Chippewa County Jail. Carl was not amused, telling the chief there'd be no more playing favorites when it came to handing out tickets, and if he ever again cost the city as much money as he did over a parking ticket, he'd have his job. While the city attorney didn't get the parking ticket he deserved, he got his comeuppance - a warning from Carl that he'd better not be seen speeding on Highway 53 when he was late for court.

While most everyone drove Highway 53 between Eau Claire and Bloomer, Chippewa Falls sandwiched between, given Grandpa's lead foot and aversion to speeding tickets, he often drove the back roads instead. My favorite, his favorite, I think, was County Highway F, which stitched together the patchwork quilt of farm fields south of Bloomer. Without the worry of getting a speeding ticket, on the hilly but about as straight a road as there was, Grandpa made better time.

Much better time. I didn't need to travel to space to experience zero gravity, if only for an instant, because getting airborne with Grandpa going over the "ticklebelly" hills on F, I'd get the same lighter-than-air feeling in my stomach I'd get riding a rollercoaster at the Northern Wisconsin State Fair. While the fair only came around once a year, Grandpa's thrill rides were year-round, lasted longer, and, best of all, were free.

There was one time, though, on July 22, 1972, when I wished Grandpa wasn't in such a hurry to get from point A to point B. Del, Ma, and I were on our way to West Salem, just east of LaCrosse, for my Uncle Mike and soon-to-be-Aunt Alice's wedding. Somewhere south of Eau Claire on Highway 53, Ma's old sky-blue Plymouth Fury III started overheating on a scorching summer day.

With steam billowing from under the hood, Del pulled off the road onto a dirt track leading down to the grass parking lot of what turned out to be a closed farm implement dealer. After lifting the hood, the three of us stared at the engine, hoping it would somehow fix itself because we couldn't. When the steam cleared and the engine still hadn't fixed itself, Del sent me up to the highway to flag down help, as family might be following us.

So I ambled up the dirt track, finding a place on the gravel shoulder where oncoming traffic could more easily see or run over me. After ten or so minutes on the lookout, I saw a fast-approaching car that looked like Grandpa's. I waved my arms with some urgency, hoping he'd see me and stop. <WHOOOOOOSH> The draft from his passing car nearly blew me off the shoulder. Back at the still broken Plymouth, I reported, "Grandpa and Grandma Wall just went by, but…"

I didn't need to finish that sentence, Ma and Del knowing Grandpa was already parking his car in the church parking lot. When we finally made it, to the wedding reception, I told Grandpa how I'd tried to attract his attention on the highway. Grandma hadn't seen me either, but then she was probably saying a Hail Mary, to herself, eyes closed, pretending to sleep… because my Grandpa Wall could fly.

057

THE LOVELY ELIZABETH

"So…" Brenda asked, "How did it go?"

"Good… I think."

"What movie did you see?"

"*The Silence of the Lambs.*"

"ON A FIRST DATE, YOU TOOK HER TO SEE *THE SILENCE OF THE LAMBS!*"

"She picked the movie."

"Oh! …sounds like your kind of girl."

From Waupaca and an undergraduate student at the University of Wisconsin-Stevens Point, those who knew her called her "The Lovely Elizabeth" …behind her back because sometimes people say nice things back there. Sorry to say, to her face, I only called her Beth.

Waitressing at the Waupaca Woods Restaurant to help pay her tuition, we met in the kitchen when I was visiting the owner and best friend, Dan. Beth was a half-sister of Corrine, she and I members of the Waupaca High School Class of 1981. Yes, I was older, not that much older, Beth not needing me to get into the R-rated *The Silence of the Lambs.* Still, it seemed strange because one of my friends mentioned Beth was just a kid when he'd go over to the house to pick up Corrine, he dating her in high school.

Beth was also a preacher's daughter - her father the pastor at the Shepherd of the Lakes Church. Fred and I were familiar with one another as he did Thursday evening summer services on the Chief Waupaca from time to time. I liked Fred. I liked Corrine. When I met Beth, I liked her too. And I guess she liked me as we went for walks several times. She liked to walk. I liked Beth. So we walked together. Her preferred paths were the winding lanes linking the homes and businesses around the Chain O'Lakes just west of Waupaca. The view was lovely. So was Beth. So was the view of Beth.

Despite all the time we spent together, we'd never been on what I'd call an actual date until we agreed to meet in Stevens Point that snowy night in February 1991. And Beth did pick the movie. I knew nothing about it. Nothing. Ab-so-lute-ly nothing. When she told me the title on the way to the theater, I thought, "*The Silence of the Lambs?* Oh boy. Sounds like a real chick flick." And in a perverse way, it was, with Jodie Foster as the story's heroine. We had plenty to talk about afterward over pizza. Plenty.

Given her choice of movie for our first date, Beth was my kind of girl, but as a psychology major, I couldn't help but think maybe, just maybe, I was a case study for one of her class projects. Either way, we both from the same cultural pool, Beth was my kind of girl in ways I wouldn't appreciate until years later. Because after Beth, a decade would pass before I'd date another Western woman - all my girlfriends in between from African or Asian countries.

Only weeks later, I was offered a teaching position at United Arab Emirates University in the desert oasis city of Al Ain. Driving 25 miles from Waupaca to Point for a date was one thing, but living in Al Ain, I'd be nine time zones removed, ten when Daylight Saving Time ended. There was no (still censored) Internet in the UAE then, and calls to the States were over two dollars per minute.

Before I moved, we shared more walks, and we'd spend the better part of another day in Point after we stopped at Hartman's Creek State Park, the beach, to go for a swim. While I could go into detail about Beth in her bikini after she sauntered out of the bathhouse, I won't. That would be inappropriate. Besides, Sue reads these stories. So does Ma.

In Point, she puttered around, ran errands, and then did some shopping, me tagging along because... did I tell you about Beth in her bikini? She called for me from a changing room in a clothing store, wanting my opinion on some blue jeans.

"Do these make my butt look big?"

"Miss Elizabeth, you're trying to seduce me, aren't you?" I said to myself.

If Beth wasn't trying to at the beach, I was sure she was at the store, and if she weren't, I'd sure like to have seen her when she was.

Tempted as I was, I did what I did best when it came to women. I played dumb. Heck, sometimes, I didn't even have to act. I didn't want to hate leaving for the UAE. I didn't want her to hate me for leaving. I hope she wasn't offended by my lack of response because if I hadn't been moving to the UAE... "Woof..."

If I have regrets, it's almost always over what I didn't do, not what I did. Maybe taking our relationship to another level would've made leaving more difficult, for the both of us, but perhaps we would've shared something we'd still remember fondly. Relationships are complex enough, never mind long-

114

distance ones, because out of sight, out of mind, people tend to move on.

That point was hammered home when I returned to Waupaca on my summer break following my first year in the UAE. Shortly before 7 am, my first morning back, I was standing in the kitchen of the Woods Restaurant, catching up with Dan while enjoying my first American restaurant breakfast in nearly a year. In the UAE, the closest I got was a British breakfast at a fancy hotel. It wasn't that close - everything supposed to be hot was cold, everything supposed to be cold was hot, and it was all greasy.

As I scarfed down my pancake - just one of Dan's enormous made-from-scratch (with his secret recipe) buttermilks enough to experience another dimension - he half-mumbled, "There's something I gotta tell you... but I can't remember what..." No sooner had I finished my pancake when Beth walked in to begin her shift. After the usual pleasantries, she held out her hand so I could get a better look... at her ring... her engagement ring.

After she moved out to the dining area, Dan turned to me and said, "Oh yeah, that's what I was gonna tell you. Beth got engaged." Even though she and I made no promises, so I had no expectations, learning of her engagement was still a punch in the gut. Good thing I'd eaten just the one pancake.

058

NOW YOU CLAP

When I was a little scrapper who didn't know he couldn't sing, I did for an audience of family and sometimes friends. With a guitar (a 1966 Christmas present, the same year I got a set of Lincoln Logs) and one foot upon a stool - probably because I saw some singer do it - I belted out songs heard on the TV, radio, or Ma's Magnavox console stereo.

One of my favorites was a song called "Duncan and Brady." A traditional murder ballad (what else would a four-year-old sing) based on events that took place in 1890 and first published in 1925, I heard it play on the Magnavox, a track on a Brothers Four album of Ma's.

Not your typical children's sing-along song, Ma says she was grateful the time I sang it for my Great Grandma Curran, that Blanche was near deaf, because the song's chorus went like this:

Oh, Brady, Brady, Brady
Don't you know you done wrong
You come into my grocery when the game was on
You sprung my lock, and you broke my door
Now you're lying dead on that barroom floor

Yup, four years old, I could remember the lyrics to adult songs (I could), sing, and play guitar (I thought I could). Ask any kid that age if they can draw, and they'll all say, "Yes!" If anyone asked me at that age if I could sing, I would've said, "Yes!" But now?

I've never done Karaoke, but if someone not knowing any better ever invited me to, and I accepted, I'd "sing" Bob Dylan's "Like A Rolling Stone" or "Subterranean Homesick Blues" because the last time I tried, I did a "good" Bob, my voice that "bad." But I like to sing, and when I do, I sing as if no one is listening because no one is - the house, car, or shower otherwise empty - I courteous to others.

I even turn up the music so I can't hear myself, my voice that bad. That doesn't mean I haven't sung in public when I was old enough to know better because I have, with an audience of 500 or so, packed into the Waupaca High School auditorium for a homecoming coronation night ceremony - free admittance, so... no refunds.

Because when I sang in public, it was for the sole purpose of getting laughs, of making a fool of myself. I wrote and then starred in three homecoming skits, only missing the fourth because Brenda invited me to be her escort on the homecoming court. My favorite skit was my take on Steve Martin's Saturday Night Live performance of his hit gag song, "King Tut." Rejiggering the lyrics, my version was titled "King Comet," Comets the school's nickname.

Other schools struggled with skits and float themes when we were their homecoming opponent because, with malice in your heart, in that context, what can you do to a comet? Really, what can you do? Compared with what you can do to a bulldog, polar bear, tiger, or, or... a penguin?

Adorned with every piece of gaudy gold-colored jewelry Ma had left from the '60s, I took the stage dressed in only a white bed sheet, "singing" the altered lyrics. Becky, a preacher's daughter, also dressed in nothing more than a white bed sheet, hand-fed me grapes between verses. I don't think her father was in the audience that night, as I would've noticed someone having a heart attack - his church known for its strict interpretation of scripture.

Fearing they'd lose to sophomores, seniors in the auditorium's control room shut off my microphone. Our class won anyway, that skit getting the loudest and longest laughs of the night, the title and visuals enough with the song still playing in the background. With my voice, those seniors probably would've been better off leaving my mic on.

Yet, as a student in that high school, when required to give an oral report for class, I was... uncomfortable, before, during, and sometimes even after. As a freshman in Mr. Adomavich's World History class, I dreaded presentation day, unable to sleep for days, unable to purposely make a fool of myself giving my report on "The Black Death," bubonic plague no laughing matter. Even so, Mr. Adomavich awarded me a good grade, suggesting my report would've been better had I begun by describing the effects of the plague on humans, you know, to grab the audience's attention. A good lesson learned.

Nervous as could be in the lead-up to giving any report in front of classmates, I knew of others with even higher anxiety, a few tempted to drop out of school to avoid the potential for embarrassment. One friend, a fellow senior, his report for a British Literature class scheduled for the afternoon, went home at lunch and had a "wee bit" to drink. I didn't see his report, but I heard he did well. Of course, this was the same friend who was tougher to beat at 8-ball later in the evening than he had been earlier - much better with a pool cue in his hand and a few drinks in him.

I enjoyed putting on a show only when free to do as I pleased. Perhaps that's why I could never put on as good of a show as Patty did for daytime tours on the Chief, the words for the tour spiel not mine, but those in a script handed to me. Looking back, I should've rewritten the information in the script and made it mine. I don't know that I would've put on a better show than Patty, but I would've put on a better show. I already looked the part of Captain John with my beard so convincing that I even had passengers reach over and tug on it.

"I just wanted to see if your beard was real."

"Yes, it's real, this isn't the Wisconsin Dells."

As Captain John, the experience of speaking with so many over so many years in so many different contexts was good practice for my next job, teaching at United Arab Emirates University. Immersed in a culture with a long oral history - lack of paper in the desert and all - they loved stories told by storytellers, and desperate for entertainment, they appreciated a good show. Why, when people asked what I did in the UAE, I told them, "I do four shows a day with matinees every other Wednesday."

After I retired, honing my showmanship in the UAE paid off as I was the top-rated speaker at 11 of the 11 conferences where I presented on behalf of a company catering to expats and wannabes, the last with nearly 1000 people in a ballroom at the Red Rock Casino in Las Vegas. I didn't sing or purposely make a fool of myself. Instead, I did what by then I knew best - I put on a good show, in my own words, spoken, not sung, backed by my photographs and a Flash video or two I created.

After a particularly emotional one-off presentation at the Swissôtel in Quito, the hundreds in attendance gave me a standing ovation, the only one anyone could remember any speaker getting in several years of the company's conferences. The only "standing-O" I've ever received, the spontaneous and emotional response - one of my most memorable moments - caught me by surprise. Enough that... those "bastards" made me cry. Why, with tears streaming down my face, I clapped back at my audience.

I'd come full circle, in a roundabout way, as Ma also tells of a family gathering at her parent's home in Bloomer, where an again four-year-old version of me stood on a piano stool singing "King of the Road," Dean Martin's version, also heard on Ma's console stereo. After I finished, I swung my arm around to include everyone in the room, declaring, "Now you clap." Ma says everyone did, including my Great Uncle George, laughing so hard tears streamed down his face.

059

MAKE A SPLASH

I knew they were watching, so walking alongside the Vilcabamba River, my eyes were searching for the biggest rock I could heave-ho, one that would make the kind of impact I was hoping for, with the river and the work crew behind me. Spotting a large, but not too large of a rock, one that would test, but not fail me, I said to myself, "That'll do, Johnny. That'll do."

My target acquired, I set my backpack on a driftwood log and leaned my pickaxe and shovel against the same before I made my way over to the rock. From a deep squat, I got a firm grip on it and then lifted with my legs - always lift with your legs. Heavier than I thought - I couldn't have lifted much more - I rested it against my chest to take some of the load off my arms as I hauled it to the river's edge, where I paused to reposition my arms... and catch my breath... before I shotput that rock into the river.

<SPLASH>

It was precisely the kind of impact I was hoping for, one that gave me instant credibility, especially since I didn't shotput my intestines out my ass. Much as I wanted to, I didn't turn around to see the reaction of the work crew behind me. I didn't have to because when that rock hit the river, I knew they knew they had the right man for the job.

It wasn't a job I'd planned on doing that day, but on an early morning river walkabout with our dog, Packers, I spotted a small group working upstream and went to investigate. I found six men - one teenager, two older than me, and three about my age, including a pair of brothers I knew a bit better than the others. While the brothers looked alike, they sure didn't act alike, as one always greeted me with a big smile and an "Ola!" whenever he passed our gate, but from the other brother, I never got more than a grudging head bob.

The work crew was re-digging the irrigation canal that ran parallel to the river just a few steps in from the riverbank. Re-digging because during the rainy season, rocks, sand, dirt, and whatever else the river pushed downstream buried the previous year's version. Extracting water from the river, the canal started on the downstream side of our property when we moved to Ecuador. During a particularly rainy rainy season that first year, the river washed out the steel-reinforced concrete mouth of the canal until it broke off.

Forever lying, cattywampus, on our river bank, Sue and I would use that pickup truck-sized chunk as a pier. And a rest stop, after river walks, there still 200 yards and 111 stairs, up, to our house. When the municipality tried and failed to reroute the river the following year, they tried and failed to move the concrete chunk. Where the river succeeded, "Miguel Mulligan and His Steam Shovel" failed.

Because the river cuts an ever-deepening path, most years, subsequent canal entrances, hand-built with rock, had to be moved further and further upstream. The canal that once started on the downstream side of our riverfront property eventually started some 200 yards upstream from there, cutting across our property in what used to be the riverbed, built up with rocks, sand, dirt, and whatever else the river pushed downstream after it defiantly chose its own route. Covered in overgrowth and dotted with some good-sized trees, you'd never know that land was where the river once was just a few years previous.

And it looked that way because, fortunately for us, most of what the river deposited on our property was dirt, same for the property just upstream from us. Beyond that, however, the river deposited rocks, lots and lots of rocks. Cutting a canal through dirt is difficult enough, but through rocks? The previous year, with a hundred or so yards of canal to re-dig through those rocks, interested residents hired a guy with a backhoe to do the job.

Getting a backhoe down to and across the river isn't always easy. While there are a few access points, the river has to be low, or it's a no-go. And if the river starts to rise, the operator better get a move on, or their expensive piece of machinery might be trapped on the wrong side of the river for weeks, maybe months, or worse, wind up downstream - what would be left of it anyway.

The municipality requires owners to maintain any irrigation canals crossing their property. Failure to do so can result in a fine equal to the cost to pay a laborer to do the job - ten dollars per day when we moved there, then twelve, then twenty. I always clean our canal, even though it's more than ten, twelve, or even twenty dollars worth of work, for me.

"Don't you have a guy for that?"

"Yes, me."

But then I do more than clean, hauling the good quality muck, judging by the stink, to build up low-lying areas on our property. It would take only half a day if I just cleaned the canal.

However, the canal near the river is not a municipal canal but private, one I'm not sure is even legal. But who would complain? Especially since it was dug and is maintained by barrio residents. The point is that no one is required to maintain it, much less dig it, as the crew was doing when I approached with a curious Packers.

Picking the friendly brother to start a conversation, in my best Spanish, I asked, "Do you want help?" careful not to ask, "Do you need help," a small but important distinction. "¡Sí! ¡Sí!" he responded with a furious head shake for emphasis that wasn't necessary because I knew the job was backbreaking work. A quick survey of the crew told me my help would indeed be appreciated, as I was at least a head taller and about half again as wide as everyone, Ecuadorians, on average, and certainly in our barrio, not the biggest people.

Not dressed for the occasion and without tools, I told the friendly brother I'd be back to help in 15 minutes. I'm not sure if he believed me, but I returned without Packers, only to find work on the canal had stopped, and the crew engaged in conversation with someone new to the party. While I was gone, the backhoe operator who'd dug the previous year's canal had heard about the community dig and made his way up the river to offer his services. Why no one noticed my arrival, they instead listening to "Captain Obvious" pitch his sale by telling the crew what they already knew - digging the canal by hand would be hard work.

I was disappointed, thinking I was about to lose my chance at neighborly team building before I even got started. Although I didn't understand every word as I listened to the negotiations, body language soon confirmed that the crew wasn't buying what the backhoe operator was selling. When they started making hand gestures - the rubbing together of thumbs and fingers - I knew they weren't buying because his price was too high.

Unable to close the deal, the frustrated backhoe owner turned and headed downstream toward Chaupi. As he passed, he gave me a look and a nod that said, "Good luck." Turning to watch him walk away, the work crew noticed I'd kept my promise to help as they saw me standing there, pickaxe in one hand, shovel in the other. Standing before me was the man in charge, Vincente, a dignified older chap I'd only ever seen wearing a fedora.

Eyeing me up, mainly because my shoulder was higher than the top of his head, a satisfied grin filled his face as he widened his stance and puffed up his chest as if to say, "Big boy. Finally, we have some size on our team!" And I was dressed to impress in my work "uniform" - Wrangler Riggs Workwear Ranger pants (Wrangler doesn't pay me for such shameless plugs, but they should), a "holy" long sleeve t-shirt so stained it could be used to administer Rorschach tests, and steel-toed work boots, always a good idea when heaving heavy rocks, especially slippery-when-wet ones.

Then there were my "tools of ignorance," as a former colleague called them. That a gringo even had such tools and knew which end to hold was probably a shock to those in the work crew who didn't know me as well as others did. That my tools were well worn, not shiny new, made a statement, as did my tattered work gloves, partly held together with duct tape.

Confident I'd established some credibility, I asked Vincente what he wanted me to do. He told me, in Spanish, of course, to work upstream, just ahead of the rest, clearing the big rocks and then using them to build up the river side of the canal that would eventually extend into the river to collect the water. Once I knew what I was expected to do, move rocks, that's when I started searching for the biggest one I could heave-ho because I knew the crew would be watching, the gringo, to see what I could, or couldn't do.

Wanting to make a splash, I let them know right from the get-go I could do the dirty work. And it was, heaving heavy rocks always is. Working like a rented mule, I thought I might pass out or do a different kind of heaving, but I didn't dare do either lest I lose all respect. Nor was I going to take a break, simply because no one else did.

I knew the rest of the crew appreciated the heavy lifting I'd done when they came along to clean out what was left. Making better-than-expected progress with my unexpected assistance, the "Big Boss Man" kept moving the finish line further upstream. I grinned at Vincente every time he did, knowing my contribution was making a difference.

After we finished the job, sometime after lunch no one ate, we made our way downstream, following the water as it filled the canal. There were handshakes and smiles all around. The great thing about either is that neither needs any translation. It was one of those moments that make living in a foreign country something special, as I'm sure my Peace Corps volunteer friends appreciate far better than I do.

As we prepared to go our separate ways, I asked the crew, in my best Spanish, "Please, next time, tell me the day before you plan on cleaning our canal. I will help. It crosses my property, too."

When we put that much work into something, it becomes "our," as I couldn't help but take some ownership. Why, whenever on a river walkabout, I check on our canal, doing what I can to keep the water flowing. Because it was a private, not a municipal canal, the work done voluntarily, no one rewarded us for our time and effort. Just knowing it was a job well done had to do.

Water had been flowing in our canal for a week or so when I ran into the brother of the friendly brother. The one who had never said a word to me in nine years, he of the grudging head bob. Our paths crossed on the Cucanama side of the suspension footbridge over the Vilcabamba River. Sitting on one of the bridge's cable anchors, he was chatting with another man as I approached. Much to my surprise, once he recognized me, I got a toothy smile, a wave, and an enthusiastic "Buenos dias!" …a reward better than any paycheck.

060

R-WOBBLE

During my first time in the Abu Dhabi Airport Cargo Village, in my second week in the UAE, I had no idea what to do, only realizing upon arrival that I had no plan to get my 17 boxes and myself back to Al Ain. Once again needing to pick up a package, you might wonder why I didn't go there again since I would've at least known my way around, sort of, instead of going to the Dubai Airport Cargo Village.

Because that would've been too easy.

That and the package was sent to my address at UAE University. What airport it landed at was a coin flip - Abu Dhabi or Dubai - this time, it came up Dubai. For my trip to Dubai, though, I was far more prepared, knowing exactly how to get there, and with my Honda finally delivered from Japan, no sitting-side-saddle bus ride would be required.

The biggest difference was that I'd be bringing help, my Arabic and English-speaking friend and colleague, Ayman. He was always up for a day out with me as it gave him another opportunity to ask more of his many questions about all things American.

Even though Al Ain was in the Abu Dhabi Emirate, Dubai was closer. And as sleepy as Dubai was pre-boom, it was at least awake, unlike Abu Dhabi. The only reason Western expats in Al Ain went to Abu Dhabi was to purchase alcohol, with a license, of course, because transporting it across emirate lines was illegal.

In my eight years living in Al Ain, I went to Abu Dhabi no more than a dozen times. When I lived in Dubai, I only went twice - the first on my second-to-last first date, the second on a field trip with students from Dubai Women's College to the Abu Dhabi airport.

Instead of picking up 17 boxes, this time there was just one, a "care package" Ma sent not via post but by air cargo. In addition to some odds and ends I no longer remember, there were a couple of boxes of Cheerios I'd use to barter with married-with-children colleagues desperate for "donut seeds." There were also a few videotapes.

That's where the problem began, as any videotape imported to the UAE was subject to confiscation. This was so the authorities could screen them to ensure no movies of "dancing girls," a sort of code for pornography, made their way into the country. When the customs officer opened my care package, he had no issue with any of the box's other contents but confiscate the videotapes he did.

"After one week, go to the Ministry of Information and Culture to collect these."

"Argh!" I didn't say that aloud because showing displeasure in such a situation would guarantee I'd be leaving with no satisfaction. Instead, I explained with all the courtesy I could muster that Ayman and I had come from Al Ain and would now have to return in another week, pleading that he let us leave with the tapes instead.

"No, only the manager can permit this, and he has gone for the day."

"Argh! Gone for the day? It's ten in the morning!" You didn't have to tell me that! That only makes it worse." Again, I kept those thoughts to myself. So Ayman took a shot at it, pleading my case in the officer's far more familiar Arabic. I stood off to the side, trying to look unperturbed, wearing my usual blue outfit for such occasions because another expat told me Arabs liked blue, making the wearer appear more honest.

After a minute or two of discussion, the officer turned to me and asked, "Who sent you these tapes?"

"My mother."

"What is on them?"

"TV shows and American football games."

"No dancing girls?"

"No, no," my reply punctuated with a smile... but not too wide of one.

He then resumed his discussion with Ayman in Arabic. After they exchanged chuckles, the officer handed me my tapes and invited me to be on my way.

"Shukran!"

Once we walked out the doors of the Cargo Village, I didn't have to ask because Ayman couldn't wait to spill his guts, "The only reason you have those tapes is because that guy thought you had an honest face!" While we both got a good laugh out of that, truth be told, I think Ayman's honest face mattered more.

A personable and exceptionally intelligent young man, I was always happy to spend time with Ayman. Good thing because, as two new guys, we shared a cubicle during our first year teaching on the Men's Campus at UAE University. The following year, however, I moved to the Women's Campus while Ayman moved to the States, where he began working on the two PhDs he earned - in electrical and computer engineering - at North Carolina State University, why he'd been so curious about all things American.

While I thought Ayman would be helpful in navigating the bureaucracy at the Cargo Village, he was, but only to a point. Even his honest face and knowledge of Arabic and English were not enough to make the experience any less exasperating. As the two of us bounced from window to window to collect my package, the process made no more sense than in Abu Dhabi, as even Ayman, an Egyptian, an Egyptian!, was shaking his head in disgust at the bureaucracy.

Just one window away from someone retrieving Ma's care package stored in the massive warehouse backing the administration building, our progress was halted at that final window by, of all things, language difficulties. Even with Ayman at my side, he was of no help because the woman behind the counter was a young Filipina who, in her best broken English, asked, "Where your R-wobble?"

"Huh?"

"R-wobble. Where your R-wobble?"

I looked at Ayman for help, but before I could ask, he asked me, "What's an R-wobble?"

"It's not an Arabic word?"

"No, I thought it was an English word I didn't know."

So I asked her to repeat what she said... more slowly.

"R-wob-ble. Where... your... R-wob-ble?"

All that succeeded in doing was to frustrate me more, more slowly. A behind-the-counter manager, an older Filipina, sensing a problem, came over to offer assistance, but after conferring with the first woman, she asked the same question, "Where your R-wobble?"

"This is not happening," I thought as Ayman and I exchanged blank stares.   No doubt they'd asked the question hundreds if not thousands of times before, but here stood an English speaker and an Arabic and English speaker, both university-educated, utterly befuddled by their request.

Ayman and I might've been standing there staring at each other all day if a man in the next queue hadn't leaned over and told us, "Airway bill. They want to see your airway bill."

"...R-wobble ...AIRWAY BILL!"

It would be the last time I collected anything at the Dubai Airport Cargo Village until ten years later when I went to pick up Tissa'a, Iqqy, and Bubbuh, my three cats, another story for another book.

061

DODGER DOGS

"All hotel rooms look the same with the lights off," said Tom Bodett in ads for Motel 6. However, there was this budget motel in Mississippi where Ma, Del, and I left the lights on after discovering the room was infested with cockroaches. There was no way we were turning out the lights at bedtime. No way.

But Tom Bodett had a point. We didn't need a fancy motel room, much less a fancy hotel room, neither of which Ma and Del could've afforded anyway. The quality of our accommodations didn't matter much because our family driving vacations were about what we saw along the way during the day, not what we saw in our room at night.

If we wanted the motel/hotel experience, we could've stayed at the Holiday Inn, with its indoor kidney-shaped pool, just down the street from Del's apartment in Eau Claire, instead of seeing much of the States and Canada. For us, a motel was simply a place to get some sleep. Since Del always liked to get an early start, sunrise, or sooner, money spent on a fancy room would've been wasted, just as Tom Bodett said.

Nevertheless, in September 1989, when I took my first solo driving trip, I preferred to stay at a Marriott.

Why not? They had a lovely continental breakfast, the public restrooms were clean and spacious, and the parking lots were lighted and often landscaped. Those factors were important to me because when I say I stayed at a Marriott, I mean I slept in a car in the parking lot as my limited budget wouldn't allow for a night at even a Motel 6.

Besides, business people stayed at Marriotts. My trip was business because, along the way, I'd be engaged in research, field study for my upcoming thesis project, "A New Stadium for Milwaukee." Yes, to do research for my Master of Architecture degree, I had, had to attend major league baseball games. While my fellow thesis students at the University of Wisconsin-Milwaukee were researching hospitals, hotels, office buildings, schools, and such, I was taking me out to the ballgame.

"Do what you love, and you'll never work a day in your life," right?

The Internet would've been mighty helpful then, as I could've learned so much more without ever leaving Milwaukee. But in 1989, as I was learning how to use my new Mac SE30 computer with 1MB of RAM and a 40MB hard drive, the Internet was still a dream for the public. Instead, I had to rely on the few books and articles about ballparks I could get my hands on.

While not an academic work, one of my favorite resources was a 1988 bestselling book by Bob Wood called *Dodger Dogs to Fenway Franks*. It was the story of his summer road trip to (at the time) all 26 Major League baseball parks. To save money on his epic journey, Bob often spent the night at a... Motel 6. Bob's book provided oodles of much-appreciated information and opinions on every stadium, but it was his storytelling that I most enjoyed.

His epic journey sounded like the kind of adventure that would provide me with an opportunity to do the see-for-myself "field study" I needed, given the dearth of hardcopy info available. The more I thought about taking my trip, the more I told myself, "You gotta do this." Now, I had neither the time nor the money to visit every major league ballpark, so I made a list of what I thought I could do with the limited time and money I had.

Fortunate to get a day off during the summer while piloting the Chief Waupaca, the only opportunity I had to make such a trip was when classes at the University of Wisconsin-Milwaukee resumed in September. Unfortunately, that was the last month of baseball's regular season, so it didn't leave me much scheduling wiggle room, especially since I figured I better attend classes the first couple of weeks so my professors wouldn't drop me from their class rosters.

First, I had to decide what ballparks I wanted to see. Having already arranged to fly to Los Angeles to visit friends Craig and Lori, I could visit two ballparks by making a trip to see Anaheim Stadium, right across the freeway from Disneyland, and another to Dodger Stadium, just north of downtown L.A.

Back in Milwaukee, I would drive, taking advantage of the shorter distances between major league stadiums in the Northeast. Tiger Stadium in Detroit? A classic must-see. Cleveland's Municipal Stadium? An old park, a big park, and on the way. OK. Pittsburgh? A multipurpose "donut" stadium? It didn't make the cut, along with those other multipurpose O's in Cincinnati, Philadelphia, and Flushing Meadows, New York. Flushing Meadows. Whenever I hear the name, I imagine a rolling field of clover sprinkled with flowers, songbirds… and glistening white toilet bowls.

Baltimore's Memorial Stadium? An underrated multipurpose stadium? Why not? Besides, Jay lived near Baltimore, and I could spend a few days visiting. New York's Yankee Stadium? Absolutely. Fenway Park in Boston? Definitely. Toronto's SkyDome? Yes! Let's make this an international trip. Besides, I could see what a retractable roof stadium was all about. They might catch on.

Since I was going to Toronto, I could stop in Buffalo to see Pilot Field, which was getting significant press for a minor-league park. And I wanted to see Chicago's other historic baseball venue, Comiskey Park, as I'd already been to Wrigley Field the previous May with friends from Waupaca. They met me in Milwaukee, and I drove us to Chicago and back, mainly because they refused to - Illinois drivers, traffic, toll gates... FIBs.

Knowing what ballparks I wanted to see, I had to devise a schedule. It wasn't as easy as it sounds because there had to be a game the day I was scheduled to be at a stadium so I could get inside. I also had to leave enough travel time to make the next game in the next city, but not so much that I'd spend time and money waiting around. And, as I learned watching one of my favorite movies, *The Bridge on the River Kwai*, there's always the unexpected, isn't there?

Despite all my planning, sure enough, before my trip even began, it was delayed as my flight from Milwaukee to Denver on the way to L.A. was canceled by a mid-September snowstorm in Colorado. There's always the unexpected, isn't there? Eventually, I got to Denver, only to discover the only flight that left Denver on time... let me repeat that... the only flight that left Denver on time was mine, to Los Angeles, just minutes after I arrived.

So I was delayed, again, the wait uncomfortable in the Denver airport as the air conditioning was still pumping cold air into the terminal, even as the snow piled up outside. But the following morning, all was well in sunny Southern California, my wardrobe far more appropriate for the weather there than it had been in Denver. And while I got to L.A. later than planned, I still had time for a good night's sleep at Craig and Lori's.

Craig kindly lent me his old Volkswagen Jetta for the drive to Anaheim for the Angels game. Much to my chagrin, I discovered his car had a manual transmission. There's always the unexpected, isn't there? Other than a one-time "experience" at Clear Water Harbor driving Pat's old Chevy pickup with three-on-the-tree, I'd never driven a vehicle lacking an automatic transmission. So that day, I learned how to drive a stick, on the L.A. freeways between the San Fernando Valley and Anaheim. If you were driving anywhere near me, I apologize.

My visit to Anaheim Stadium confirmed what I'd already suspected - football had ruined "The Big A." Once a pristine baseball-only park, it had been awkwardly altered into a multi-purpose stadium to host the football Rams after they left their longtime home at the L.A. Coliseum. Like the cafegymatorium at Westwood Elementary in Waupaca, the new Anaheim Stadium was ideally suited for... nothing. To make matters worse, to accommodate the additional seating for football, The Big A, the iconic scoreboard and inspiration for the stadium's nickname, had been banished to the parking lot.

Baseball wasn't the only attraction that night, though, as a group of celebrity lookalikes roamed the ballpark, mingling with fans. C'mon, Angels, with

Hollywood just up the freeway, you couldn't get the real deals? Maybe the real deals went to Dodger games… as fans. The only celebrity lookalike I remember was Kim Basinger.

For some context, three years earlier, the steamy movie *9½ Weeks* was released starring the sultry Ms. Basinger, the real one, when I was a 23-year-old male… with a pulse. At the Angels game that night, Kim's doppelgänger was close enough that a guy could dream… until I saw her in the upper deck concourse engaged in a heated argument with what appeared to be a jealous boyfriend, and the dream was gone.

I can still see her in that little black dress…

But I digress…

As for my wardrobe, I was dressed as I always was when I toured a stadium - in blue jeans, a t-shirt, a travel vest, a jacket, a camera bag over my shoulder, and a notebook and pen in hand. Like fake Kim Basinger's little black dress, my outfit no doubt helped me get into places I typically couldn't because I looked the part of something. So much so one kid at Anaheim Stadium walked up to me and asked, "Are you a reporter for the *L.A. Times*?"

"Why, yes. Yes, I am. Got a story for me, kid?"

He scurried away.

As was true at every ballpark I visited, I couldn't go everywhere I wanted, but I pushed the limits as much as possible to access areas normally off-limits to spectators. In addition to my "uniform," projecting an attitude that said I belonged, even when I didn't, also proved helpful.

"What are you doing here?"

"Research."

With that confident response, peppered with just the right amount of disdain, security guards usually let me get on with my work. At Detroit's Tiger Stadium, one appreciated my breaking up the monotony of his guarding nothing in particular to give me a tour. There's always the unexpected, isn't there? I bought him a bratwurst for his trouble. It seemed the Milwaukee thing to do.

Yankees 3
Angels 4
Attendance – 30,670

I was off for a much-anticipated day game at Dodger Stadium the following morning. There wasn't much to see from the outside - Dodger Stadium built into the ground at Chavez Ravine. The Sulfur and Cemetery Ravines were cut and filled to level the surrounding area for parking. The Palo Verde elementary school, located outside the left field stands, was buried under some of the eight million cubic yards of dirt that were moved to build Dodger Stadium.

But from the inside of Dodger Stadium, there was plenty to see in addition to the stadium and the game - the San Gabriel Mountains behind the outfield fence, the Hollywood sign beyond the left field foul pole, and behind home plate, from the concourse on the top level where I was seated, the smoggy skyline of downtown Los Angeles.

Having read the book, I had to try a Dodger Dog. I think the wiener makers in Milwaukee would've approved, so I had a couple-two-three more, helped by the fact there were no lines at the concession stands as a smog alert on the muggy 92-degree day kept attendance down. However, the lack of fans was disappointing because I learned more by observing a stadium working at or near capacity. Instead, I was part of the smallest crowd for a Dodgers home game in 13 years.

At least I made it to the game. While somewhat more comfortable driving a stick on the second day, the entry to the Dodger Stadium parking lot was... challenging, as the gates were near the top of a quarter-mile-long incline. When I arrived, early, there were no other cars in sight - perhaps an L.A. first - for which I was grateful because after I paid the attendant, I couldn't get Craig's Jetta into first gear while pointed uphill. I sheepishly explained to the man that it was my friend's car, and I was not used to driving a stick.

After a few more failed attempts to get it in gear, I asked the parking attendant to "Keep the gate open!" I then threw the Jetta into reverse and proceeded to execute a backward Y-turn, shifting the car into first gear as I headed forward downhill. Once in first gear, I loopy-looped the Jetta uphill and zipped through the open gate, smiling and waving as I passed the attendant, laughing hysterically with a story he would no doubt tell later that day, probably more than once.

Astros 11
Dodgers 3
Attendance - 13,206

062

THANKFULLY, NO TRAIN

Between the top and "THAT WAS AWESOME!" State Street's hill lacked the STOP signs, railroad tracks, too-tight turns, or pedestrians that littered other hilly streets in Eau Claire. Why the hill on the city's south side was the only one I ever went down on my bike at full speed... on purpose anyway.

To get a flying start, I'd time the traffic light at the intersection above the hill, giving me a few blocks on the flat to build up speed before beginning my descent. While the hilly part of the street had been resurfaced and widened, making for a smooth run with some elbow room, State Street narrowed considerably in a residential neighborhood after the thrill was gone.

With tree-lined streets and dignified older homes, the neighborhood had character. At the bottom of the hill, State Street did, too, the newer paving giving way to older asphalt with numerous potholes, bumps, and cracks. Only once did I make the mistake of keeping my butt on my bicycle seat when I got to the end of a State Street hill gravity run.

Until it wasn't, the State Street hill was fun and fast, even if the posted speed limit was just 30mph. Jay once told me he was about halfway down on his ten-speed bike when a man pulled alongside in a car, lowered the power window on the passenger side, looked at his dashboard, then looked back at Jay and shouted, "50 miles per hour!"

Such speed was not possible on the Dewey and Madison Street hills because the two streets crossed about halfway down a hill in one of the wonkiest intersections in Eau Claire. What made the crossing truly wonky, though, were the four railroad tracks that intersected that intersection at another angle.

Dewey Street was quiet - the railroad tracks probably saw more action - but Madison Street was always busy as the primary connector between the city's elevated north side and downtown. That's why what little traffic there was on Dewey Street faced a STOP sign at the intersection, while drivers on Madison Street didn't have to stop unless there was a train, and there could be more than 30 traffic-stopping trains per day.

Pulling into or out of the rail yard serving the Uniroyal Tire plant one block east, the trains were always slow rollers and almost always long. Stuck at the crossing counting cars, my tally often reached triple digits, so delays too would be long, get-out-of-your-car-and-chat-with-others-stuck-at-the-crossing long. Why I figure I'm owed a few extra days in my life, given how much time I spent facing uphill or downhill on Madison Street waiting for the caboose and a wave from the rear brakeman seated inside.

With the first train arriving in Eau Claire in 1870, how the placement of train tracks would affect not-yet-invented cars was of no concern. By the early 1900s, though, there was talk of building a tunnel on Madison Street under the tracks. Talk progressed to building plans and a May Day 1915 completion deadline, but construction never started - no explanation given.

Instead, the building of a bridge, not a tunnel, wouldn't begin until 1977, the project finally completed in 1978, 63 years late… later.

Dewey Street now double dead ends on each side of Madison Street and the bridge. Where once there were four railroad tracks, now there's only one (and a trail). Passing under the bridge, traffic on Madison Street is no longer stuck waiting for far fewer trains after Uniroyal, once America's third-largest tire plant, closed in June 1992. Figures. When I lived there, when Uniroyal was cranking out tires in three shifts, there was no bridge, but after I moved away…. Watching the trains, though, I learned to count to 100, with every count ending, "CABOOSE!"

In the summer of 1975, two years before bridge construction began, Ma, Del, Jay, and I were living on Eau Claire's south side, Ma and me just for the summer, Del and Jay full-time. But Del's parents, Elmer and Erna, still lived on the north side. Angels that we were, Jay and I rode our bikes over to pay regular visits. After an afternoon of cutthroat canasta with Erna, it was time to head home.

There were two ways to go. The shorter route was down to downtown, then up either State Street or Garfield Avenue hills. The longer but mostly level way home was going around downtown on some of Eau Claire's busiest thoroughfares. Jay had just turned 20, seven years older than me, so it was his call. He chose the more direct route, leading the way over the top of the Dewey Street hill, downtown at the bottom.

Riding the brakes on my new ten-speed bike, I took it slow, knowing we'd have to stop halfway down because of the traffic on Madison Street. Trailing Jay by half a block as he approached Madison Street and the railroad crossing, I was puzzled as to why he was not slowing or stopping but speeding up. I then watched in disbelief as Jay threaded the needle through cross traffic, unscathed, as I'd only seen in cartoons.

"I suppose if Jay rode straight through a busy intersection over railroad tracks, you'd do it too?"

As a matter of fact, mothers everywhere, I would and did, also without incident. But same as Jay, not without a close call or two and horn-honking from startled drivers. Thankfully, no train...

Jay weaved back and forth down the lower half of the Dewey Street hill, almost as devoid of traffic as the upper half. A block past the bottom, he rolled to a stop. When I caught up with him, he was leaning against a parked car, recombobulating.

"Are you insane?" I exclaimed, even though I'd just done the same thing, but since I was following the leader, the adult, my on-the-spot analysis was that Jay was the crazy one.

To answer my question, he reached under his handlebars and held up a broken cable, "No brakes... and I was going too fast to stop."

"Ahhh jeez."

"Don't you dare tell Pa or your mother the truth."

As you know, not the first time Jay told me that. Still not the last, either.

063

FINDING OUT ABOUT HER

She was on the other end of the longest telephone call I've ever been a part of, eight hours, yet the first time I met her, I was something I rarely am - speechless. As she went down the line exchanging greetings with my colleagues, by the time she got to the end, me, even though she only said, "Hello," that was one more word than I managed. Standing at the end, I had time to think of something to say, but...

As you may have guessed, I met a girl, but not just any girl, a young lady from Egypt, one of those rare people I remember meeting for the first time, this time, in the United Arab Emirates University Women's Campus Library. The first time ever I saw her face, peeking out from her headscarf, there was a sparkle in her eyes... and when she smiled her smile... just one look was all it took...

Despite our one-word first encounter, we'd be talking for hours in a matter of days, highlighted by our all-night talkathon. That call ended only because her family began to rise with the sun, so we had to call it a night. That's how many of our conversations ended - because they had to, not because we wanted them to - we always had so much more to say.

Her first language Arabic, she once apologized for her deficiencies in English. After I stopped laughing, I told her, "Your English is better than mine!"

After she stopped laughing, she asked, "Gosh, you really think so?"

"Yes, I do." And I said it because I meant it, she one of the most articulate people I've ever met, even though she spoke to me in a language far different from her own. With just one word - gosh - she could express so much in the way she'd say it, whether as a noun, verb, adjective, adverb, interjection, or exclamation. Her words filled my ears so I could hear nothing else, but not so full it pained me. Hypersensitive to sound, that mattered, I passing on women I otherwise liked because their voices scratched my eyeballs, from the inside. "I'm not listening to that for the rest of my life."

I wish I'd met her sooner, as I was seemingly the only one at work who'd not yet had the pleasure. Everyone spoke so highly of her, some with a level of reverence I'd never before heard any man talk about any woman or any woman talk of another woman. I was well into my first semester at UAEU when I finally met her and saw for myself the young lady everyone spoke about in such glowing terms.

Unable to stop thinking about her after our Wednesday (Friday) afternoon meeting, hours later, her brother and I were at a club in the InterCon Hotel. While we were colleagues, in the weeks we'd worked together and gotten to be friends, he'd never mentioned his sister. After meeting her, I understood why. I wouldn't want my friends to know she existed if she were my sister. Especially that one friend, you know the type.

Surrounded by women dancing to the latest beat and the men hounding them, I thought only of her. I had to say something to her brother. I had to, even though I knew I shouldn't. While waiting for an opening to say what I shouldn't, I considered a number of options, none that included keeping my mouth shut. When my opening came, I went with, "I met your sister today."

All the nice things I then said about her, or how nicely I said them, didn't matter because I'm sure all her brother heard was, "I want to violate your sister in a dozen different ways." His unease with my meeting his younger sister was no reflection on me, he was just protective of her, especially knowing the attention she attracted, without even trying.

His attitude made more sense later after I learned it was not so much Muslim fathers the problem, but brothers who knew what their friends were like and how they talked about women. Not that I ever talked like that in front of her brother or anyone. Still, I could tell he'd rather I said nothing... because he told me so.

Every unmarried man, probably a few married ones, hoped to be the guy who caught her eye, including me. Typically struggling to strike up a conversation with a woman who caught my eye, I often said nothing, but so enamored with her, I knew I'd never forgive myself if I didn't at least try.

Despite my failure to get so much as a word out when we met - just a smile and a nod - I fared much better on subsequent encounters, mostly because she made it easy. Is it possible? Do I dare think it? That maybe, just maybe, she was interested in me too? Then she started making excuses to be near me as I did to be near her, and I knew what I hoped was true.

After a few exchanges, we started calling each other at work once we knew each other's schedule. Never having enough time, you know, work always interrupting, I gave her my home phone number so we could talk more. I already had her home number from calling her brother, but I couldn't call her. Now, if I was calling him and she happened to pick up… After a conversation as long as she felt we could get away with, we'd hang up, and I'd call again. She'd answer. We'd giggle. Then she'd shout, "Brother! It's for you!"

Without landline telephones, our relationship probably wouldn't have gone far, most of our quality time confined to phone conversations, although I walked her home from work a few times. Well, close to home, as my walking her to her door wouldn't have gone over so well with her family. Probably. We, especially she, maybe me, didn't want to find out.

It was the same the few times I drove her home, dropping her off around the corner, out of sight from her villa. She navigated during the drive since she knew the rules of "the game" far better than I did. Much to my delight, she never chose the shortest route to her home, and I countered by never questioning why. For example, when she'd have me drive around the park… again… and again… and again… to extend our precious time together.

Difficult as it was, we did our best while keeping up appearances by pretending to barely know each other when we were together in front of others, at work, or in social settings. To avoid scandal, we had to because, in the UAE, there was no acceptable reason we should be so familiar.

I couldn't tell anyone of our relationship, even though I wanted to shout it from the rooftop, any rooftop, every rooftop. I likened it to having an affair, all the sneaking around, and not being able to tell anyone. Two of her female friends knew, but I knew I didn't dare tell any of my male friends.

The only time she seemed unconcerned about what others might think was at a New Year's Eve party at her family's villa, as she sat on the sofa next to me, much to the chagrin of almost every man there, including her brother.   With my friends either not there or in Thailand during the holiday break, I was relieved I wouldn't have to explain her interest, perhaps why she showed some, publicly.

After meeting her, and especially after we'd made a connection, my feet didn't touch the ground when I walked.   I looked forward to every day like I never had before, dumbstruck at my good fortune in finding her, a woman unlike any other I'd ever met, and all I had to do was move halfway around the world.   Then, one day at work, I got to talking with a colleague, and we got to talking about her.

"You know who she is, right?"

"Obviously, I know who her brother is."

"No, no, I mean, do you know who her father is?"

"Her father? No."

You know those movies where the clueless guy finds out a little too late that he's dating the boss's daughter? Or the dean's daughter? Yeah... if not for my best poker face, my colleague would've discovered what I just had - that I was both of those guys.

064

IT WAS THE COMMERCIALS

"Unka John! Time for *The Smurfs*!"

Preceded by a bop on the head, that was my reveille many a Saturday morning living in Gainesville. It wouldn't have been so bad, except I worked from 3 pm Friday until 3 am Saturday at a place called Beerworld, a gas station, car wash, and convenience store. By the time I got home, watched a little late-night TV, and then got to bed, I hadn't been asleep long before it was time for *The Smurfs*, you know, those little blue people you heard so much about.

Jay and Jean both worked early Saturday mornings. So, as soon as Jayme woke up, I was on the babysitting clock. Not long after she woke up, realizing her parents were gone, she knew it must be Saturday. As far as Jayme was concerned, I'd had a good night's sleep. I had not, but she was up and wanted me to be, too, mostly so I could turn on the TV. She was not allowed to touch the TV, mostly because two-year-olds tend to spend most of the day with their hands covered in something sticky.

"Jayme, I know you know how to turn on the TV. Go turn it on, watch *The Smurfs*."

"No, Unka John. Can't touch TV."

It didn't stop her from touching the TV. She knew how to turn it on, change the channels, and adjust the volume. But she played by the rules on Saturday mornings, mainly because it would get me out of bed so she'd have some company while she did everything but watch *The Smurfs*. So even though it was the last thing I wanted to do, I'd stumble out to the living room and turn on the TV.

"What channel is *The Smurfs* on?

"That one Unka John."

"OK."

Then *The Smurfs* came on. The first time I saw the show, I thought it was just my lack of sleep, but they appeared to be blue. They also had squeaky voices, just what I wanted to hear on almost no sleep after working a 12-hour shift. With *The Smurfs* on, I'd find a place on the sofa and try, and fail, to stay awake, believing whatever Jayme was going to do wouldn't involve playing with matches or running with scissors. I didn't really care if she touched the TV, as long as she didn't break it.

I was never asleep for long before I'd get another bop on the head, "Unka John, I want breffast." No doubt she'd seen a commercial for some sugary kids' cereal on TV, and since I was sleeping, she must've figured it was the perfect time to ask. Even though it was the last thing I wanted to do, I'd stumble out to the kitchen.

"What kind of cereal do you want?"

"That one!"

I filled Jayme's bowl with Fruit Loops and milk. It looked like wapatuli barf, just what I wanted to see on almost no sleep after working a 12-hour shift. So we'd head back to the living room, me setting her cereal bowl on the coffee table to prevent any accidents in transit.

Jayme was a picky eater with eyes bigger than her stomach. She asked for a lot but often only ate a little before abandoning it. Warm, soggy Fruit Loops. Lovely. Fortunately, I usually missed a second look at the bowl of technicolor barf, waking up just in time to see Minnie the cat finishing it - she then spending the morning doing laps around the apartment, on the walls.

Sprawled out on the sofa, my feet propped up on the coffee table, I'd get my second wind, eventually. Awake but in a daze, I still noticed something. Jayme seldom actually watched TV, the shows anyway, but when the commercials came on, she'd stop whatever she was doing, put Dolly down, and, in a rare display of focus for a two-year-old, she'd watch intently.

Commercials? Really? I'd always thought them annoying unless I needed to go to the bathroom, get something to eat, or stop the bleeding. But here was this two-year-old girl, mesmerized with what corporate America was trying to sell, and on Saturday mornings in particular, with cartoons on, trying to sell her.

I started paying attention when I was home during the week because, Monday through Friday, we babysat for another two-year-old girl, Alicia. Sure enough, the two of them would play during late afternoon cartoon time, ignoring the idiot box until a commercial came on. They'd stop what they were doing to watch "Short Attention Span TV," but as soon as the show returned, they went back to playing.

Fascinating…

Even more fascinating was that years later, I came to love those commercials I'd almost always found so annoying. Only after I'd moved to Al Ain, where TV was slim pickings at best, available only through "rabbit ears" or an aerial. Abu Dhabi 2 broadcast in English most evenings, and Dubai 33's programming was almost all in English during the evening - if, and that was a big if - I could get decent reception. I'd come full circle from my days in Eau Claire, as I only had one channel, two on a good day.

Programming was limited to a few hours per day, closing with the UAE national anthem - when's the last time you saw a TV station sign off with a national anthem? The shows left something to be desired as the daytime soap *The Bold and The Beautiful* was the heart of prime-time viewing. You read that right, *The Bold and The Beautiful*. The first couple of years, it was followed by then twenty-year-old reruns of... *Falcon Crest*.

During my first year teaching evenings on the Women's Campus, my students couldn't get out the door fast enough at the end of the class.

"*Falcon Crest* comes on at 8, sir."

"You watch that? It's 20 years old."

"Good show, sir."

"OK... You know that older lady? She was President Reagan's first wife."

"She look just like his wife now, sir."

"Yes... yes, she does."

After *Falcon Crest* finished, on came the local news from Abu Dhabi. It didn't matter what the day's news was, as every broadcast started with these words, "His Highness The President Shaikh Zayed bin Sultan al Nahyan..." The Michelin Man could've destroyed France in a drunken rampage. Scientists could've found a cure for cancer. Martians could have invaded Earth. It wouldn't have mattered. The news still would've started with these words, "His Highness The President Shaikh Zayed bin Sultan al Nahyan..."

But thanks to the local news, in English, I got to know my Shaikhs, even if I learned little else about the day's events.   The local stations also broadcast commercials, between shows, but once a show started, they rarely interrupted.   However, the evening call to prayer could, would, and often did cut off an actor mid-sentence. Muslims could wait to do a prayer as long as they completed it before the next, but such was not the case for the fifth and final one - the evening prayer.

With so little to watch before the UAE government legalized satellite TV and the (still censored) Internet, I started importing my TV. Back in Wisconsin during my summer break, I made it easier for Ma to send me recorded TV by purchasing a case of 10-hour VHS tapes. Each week, she was to fill a tape with "quality" American TV programming from a list of shows I left her. I also purchased specially made VHS tape mailers, which I addressed and affixed proper postage to, so all she needed to do was pop in a tape, seal the box, and drop it in a mailbox.

During football season, she was to devote three or so hours recording Green Bay Packers football games. I wouldn't see them for a month or two, after the Ministry of Information and Culture had a chance to screen the tapes in case they contained counterculture programming. Yes, in the UAE, it was some man's job to fast-forward through videotapes searching for nudity.

Some of my colleagues also imported their TV, having family or friends record and mail it to them. Some recorders, thinking they were doing the recipient a favor, would do so as they watched the programs, pausing the recording during commercial breaks. No one faulted their intent, as cutting out the commercials saved time for the actual shows, and given how many commercials there are, a lot of time.

At least they help pay for TV, although less than they used to because shows used to take up at least 27 minutes of a 30-minute time slot. Now it's sometimes less than 20 minutes. Airing reruns of older (longer) shows, networks overlap the credits to gain time. They also speed up playback ever so slightly to make them fit, sometimes even editing out parts deemed irrelevant.

However, much to the amazement of those doing the recording, they were thanked for being so thoughtful not to record the commercials and then told, "Don't do that again!" Because the commercials made us feel we were watching TV from home. They were a window to American "culture," slickly packaged in 30 and 60-second increments. So, in addition to kids and corporations, add expats to the short list of those who like commercials.

Here in Ecuador, I seldom watch "live" TV, mostly only when I'm watching sports, as Sue and I normally watch streaming or downloaded shows, so there are no commercials. But when I'm streaming a game, I see those commercials enough to know what matters to Americans - pizza, money, insurance, smartphones, pickup trucks, and drugs… sorry… pharmaceuticals. I don't know how those advertisers do it, but I sure get a hankering for pizza, even after I've just eaten pizza.

Fascinating…

065

ROCK AND ROLL

"Wait 'til you get back to the States. It'll seem like every driver is on Valium." Told to me less than a month into my first year at United Arab Emirates University by a colleague with a year's experience, I didn't appreciate the insightfulness of his remark, but I would, after I'd seen it for myself. Which I did, in the States on summer break following my first year in the UAE, after Ma picked me up at the Outagamie County airport just west of Appleton, Wisconsin.

Heading west on Highway 10 toward Waupaca, it didn't take long before I wondered, "Why is Ma driving so slow? C'mon Ma, I go faster backing out of my driveway in Al Ain." Was Ma popping little yellow pills? The subject of the 1966 Rolling Stones song, "Mother's Little Helper," highlighting the sudden popularity of calming drugs taken by housewives and the potential hazards of overdose or addiction.

Before I could believe Ma had started popping pills, I looked at the speedometer - 60mph. The speed limit was 55mph. The voice inside my head? That of my colleague, for as I looked around at the traffic, it did indeed seem like every driver was on Valium as they all appeared to be driving in slow motion.

In the UAE, traffic accidents were the second leading cause of death. Heart attacks were first. My theory? Most heart attacks resulted from driving in the UAE. Almost every street looked like a racetrack as municipal workers painted the curbs in alternating black and white stripes. All that was missing was a Start/Finish line and a couple of overeager kids squeezing the controls to make the cars go as fast as possible - those of you who had a slot car racing set when you were young will understand.

Following my return to the States, driving required some adjustment because on the back streets of Waupaca, where the speed limit was 25mph, I found myself doing 50mph, and it still felt like I was the one popping those little yellow pills. After less than a year of driving in the UAE, I was amazed at how my perspective had changed because in Al Ain, with its three lanes in each direction, date palm-lined boulevard streets connected by large roundabouts, driving was a breeze. More a <WHOOSH> as I could do, and sometimes did do 90mph on city streets, downtown. Out on the city's edges or on the highways, the only reason I didn't go faster was that my Honda Civic couldn't.

During my first year there, my daily commute to the Men's Campus, located on the edge of the downtown core, was uninterrupted, except for one stop-and-go light in front of Al Jimi Hospital. "Who put that there?" Sure, there were roundabouts along the way, but the right-left-right swerving through them broke up the monotony of the straightaways.

Starved for entertainment, I turned my commute into a game of "beat the clock." Sort of. With no clock in the car and me never wearing a watch, I instead timed my drive with a mixed tape I made specifically for driving around Al Ain.   The first song on Side A, fittingly, was Led Zeppelin's "Rock and Roll," the dashboard-banging tune three minutes and forty seconds long, my commute, slightly less than three miles long.

I'd pop in the tape, hit Play, and see if I could make it to work before Robert, Jimmy, John, and John Paul finished.   I had to average 50 mph to beat the clock. Don't forget, there was always that pesky stop-and-go light - the red light lit around half the time. If 50mph doesn't sound all that fast, I pressed Play before I backed out of my driveway, and to beat the clock, "Rock and Roll" had to be still playing after I parked in the campus lot.

Even so, I almost always "won," usually listening to the boys finish up while sitting in the university's parking lot, energized and ready for work. While my Grandpa Wall had a lead foot, I had a Led Zeppelin… song.

066

I'M NOT EATING THAT

Listeners of Del's morning talk show on WOKL Radio in Eau Claire sent him many a good recipe, but I swear some, seemingly more dare than delicious, were sent in by a crazy old lady living in a house full of cats. "Fluffy, let's see if mommy can get Dial Del to eat this…"

Over the years, I've gotten good at determining whether a recipe would produce a meal I'd eat. Sue too, as she'll show me a recipe and ask, "Would you eat this? Seems like you would." Most of the time, she's right. If not, it's because she's found a recipe with a reason for why not we've not yet encountered in our years together.

When our time together started including home-cooked meals, one of the first things Sue learned was not to prepare anything that included mushrooms. Not only do I despise their look, taste, and feel, I'm not eating anything grown in the Devil's basement.

After I moved to Ecuador, one of the first Spanish phrases I learned was "sin champiñones" (without mushrooms) after unknowingly ordering a pizza that included them. Even though the mushrooms hid amongst the pizza's other toppings, my gag reflex found them, "No problemo."

When I was a kid, despite my dislike, Ma insisted on drowning various dishes in Campbell's Cream of Mushroom soup. Her solution to my mushroom aversion? "Just pick them out." In an effort to get me to eat mushrooms, she once tried to convince me that she made French toast, one of my favorites, with cream of mushroom soup.

"Ma, as you know, I was born at night, but not last night."

My refusal to eat toe-mold helped get me labeled a fussy eater. Fussy? Even though I happily ate all my vegetables, including spinach. Fussy? Even though I'd eat any, any cut of steak put in front of me, as long as it wasn't covered in mushrooms, sautéed, as if that somehow made them less gag-inducing. Fussy? I preferred the term discerning. If only Ma'd known then that there'd come a day when I'd eat camel at a wedding reception... and enjoy it.

I knew what I liked and what I didn't. Another thing I didn't was Ma's baloney, noodle, and corn casserole. I like baloney. I like noodles. I like corn. Just don't mix them all together because "I'm not eating something that looks like someone already did."

At least Del was on my side on that one, as he wouldn't eat it either. Like me, he didn't even want to be in the house when baloney, noodle, and corn casserole was about because the smell... was... just... So Ma usually made it for herself when Del and I were away, for an extended period, so there'd be no leftovers lurking when we returned.

Moreover, what I don't eat, like mushrooms, I won't eat, not even to be a polite dinner guest. Wouldn't you rather feed your dog what I left on my plate than have me gagging, or worse, at your dinner table? I thought so. A friend of Ma's loved sauerkraut, a Wisconsin "delicacy." I hated the stuff. So did Ma. While the smell alone could knock a buzzard off a cabbage wagon, Ma told me I had to eat it to be polite. Polite? If her friend had any manners, she wouldn't be serving us rotten cabbage for dinner.

So I buried my kraut in leftover mashed potatoes, spread the pile around the plate so it didn't look so much, and then claimed I was full, hoping not to arouse suspicion because Ma knew I loved mashed potatoes. What choice did I have after her friend's dog turned up her nose at the sauerkraut? Poodles are fussy like that.

Eating at someone else's home is a crapshoot, even as an adult. Unless it's dinner at the home of my friends Dan and Marsha because I know what I'm going to get there - pizza delivery, sin champiñones, or some form of grilled meat, with potatoes, buns, salad, and corn, always corn... all served separately, including dessert, and it's all gonna be good! Really good!

Dinner at home is always a sure thing, too, as any meal Sue prepares is one I'll not only eat but also enjoy. There's no picking out fungi or eating rotten cabbage, just to be polite. And if Sue wants something for dinner that I don't, like chicken pot pie - another dish that looks pre-eaten - she makes it for herself, and I make something else. And of course, when I do the cooking, I won't make something I won't eat.

But Ma and Del did. Looking back, I probably should've gone along and supervised on Saturday mornings when they did the grocery shopping - kept those cream of mushroom soup cans out of the shopping cart. Although I always helped unpack the grocery bags when they returned home, mainly to see what would be on the menu for the coming week.

One Saturday morning, I unpacked a one-pound package of ground beef, a box of Ore-Ida tater tots, and a couple of cans of Green Giant French-cut green beans. Ma and Del informed me we'd have all three items for dinner. Figuring it would be cheeseburger and tater tot night, I was in a particularly good mood that afternoon. So good, I even cleaned my room, a bit, without anyone asking (telling) me to.

However, when the call came for dinner, I saw a nine-by-nine-inch cake pan in the middle of the kitchen table... and nothing else.

"What is it?"

"Dinner."

"What is it?"

"Del got this recipe from a listener."

"What is it?"

"Tater tot casserole."

"Ah, geez..."

I didn't need to see the recipe to know the supposedly responsible adults I was taking life cues from had mixed the ground beef and green beans with, let me guess, a can or two of cream of mushroom soup, plopped it in the cake pan, then covered their crime with crumbled tater tots before baking it.

"I'm not eating that."

"But it's made with things you like!"

"Not all mixed together."

"But it all gets mixed together in your stomach."

"I don't taste it in my stomach."

"It isn't that bad."

"Oh yes, it is!"

"How do you know you don't like it if you don't at least try some?"

"I don't have to put my hand in a fire to know I'll get burned."

Ma cut the casserole into nine squares, then placed one piece on Del's plate, then another on hers. It looked even worse than I imagined, the layer under the crumbled tater tots resembling the sludge I'd find cleaning the drain trap under the kitchen sink. Then Ma put a piece on my plate.

"Just taste it."

"I'm not eating that."

"Just try some."

"No."

"You're not leaving the table until you do."

Challenge accepted! So I sat there, watching Ma and Del eat what could've, should've been the best meal all week. Even though six pieces remained, neither Ma nor Del took seconds because I knew that they knew what I already knew - their tater tot casserole was disgusting. I went to bed hungry a time or two when I was a kid, but never enough to have eaten that slop.

When they'd had enough, probably after one bite, not that they'd ever admit it, they cleared their dirty dishes. All that remained on the table was a still life - my plate, topped by one untouched piece of tater tot casserole, framed by a fork, a knife, a spoon, and the glass of milk that turned out to be my dinner that night.

Ma reminded me, "You don't leave this table until you try some," she and Del then made their way to the living room to watch TV. Sitting just a few feet away, not only did I not eat their tater tot casserole, but I did the best impression of the Lincoln Memorial they'd ever see, even after the 10 o'clock news finished and Ma and Del went to bed.

It wasn't until an hour later, when I was sure they were asleep, that I finally got up from the table, six hours after I first sat down, and went to bed. I left the light on over the table, spotlighting my empty glass of milk and the untouched piece of what was for dinner.

That was the last I ever saw of that tater tot casserole. Ma and Del never made it again. And the leftovers? They mysteriously disappeared. In case you're wondering, we did not have a dog. Nevertheless, tater tot casserole night wasn't a total loss because Ma and Del finally learned I mean what I say when I say, "I'm not eating that."

067

BAD HORSE

A split nationality household, deciding which country would be our last came down to two countries - the United States and Canada. We could move to either without much fuss, certainly less than was required of us to move to the United Arab Emirates and then Ecuador. Since we'd be senior citizens, what it came down to, primarily, was in one country, half of us would have immediate health care just for being Canadian, while the other half, as her husband, would soon be eligible. In the other country, neither of us would have health insurance on the first or last day unless we bought it, assuming we could afford it. So... Canada.

Living in Ecuador would've been good practice for living in the States because we've never had health insurance here. Here, that isn't such a big deal - health care far cheaper than what we couldn't afford in the States. Not having health insurance is still a roll of the dice, but thanks to a horse, the one time we would've used it, we really didn't need it.

Pamela, a friend of ours, had a horse and invited us to join her and her husband, Mel, for a midday ride. We accepted. We wouldn't have to go far to saddle up, the horses kept in a stable at the live end of our dead-end dirt (we aspired to gravel) road, taken care of by a horse trainer gent named Juan who has passed our property on his prized horse many a time.

We drove up to the stable, meeting up with Pamela and Mel, then began what would be a four-hour ride by clip-clopping down our road, passing by our property. A few minutes later, we crossed the footbridge over the Vilcabamba River, connecting the barrios of Chaupi and Cucanama. The horses had done the crossing many times, so they weren't spooked. Good because sitting atop a horse trotting over the narrow footbridge, we were above the railing, the river a fair fall, the water not that deep, littered with concrete chunks of old bridges. We made it across without incident, why that's not the story.

After riding our way around Mandango Mountain, then the fringes of Vilcabamba, we found ourselves back on the main (only) road between Loja and Vilcabamba, within sight of the stable, atop a hill above the highway, the almost end of what had been a pleasant day. My horse was pokey, as I was always bringing up the rear, which gave me more time to take pictures, my Nikon slung around my neck, so I didn't mind. Pam and Mel were first to make the left onto our dead-end dirt road, Sue a few trots behind, and me, many more. Once Pam and Mel's horses hit the dirt road, they knew they were almost home and made a break for it.

Sue's horse, not yet on the dirt road, but seeing the other horses galloping off full speed, took off. The difference? Sue's horse had yet to make the left turn. Which it did, but Sue did not. Thrown from her horse as it leaned into the corner, she landed, fortunately, on the dirt road, not the asphalt highway. Trailing behind, I knew something had happened, but the brush along the highway blocked my view of Sue and her horse.

As I made the left turn, my horse still poking along, I saw Sue lying in a proverbial heap in the middle of the road. Her horse was fine and back at the stable by the time I reached the scene. Sue sat upright, shaken from the fall, as was I. Even though she assured me she was OK, my first question was, "Did you hit your head?" She said, "No," but the bump I felt on the back of her head said, "Yes."

A pickup driven by a known local just happened to come along. Already pointed in the right direction, I flagged him down, then helped Sue into the pickup for the ride up the hill toward town, the hospital almost within sight. It's emergencies like these when knowing some Spanish came in handy because "HELP-O!" wouldn't get it done.

After returning my horse to the stable, I followed behind a few minutes later in the FJ. Even so, our man, Eugenio, a local taxi driver, beat me to the hospital - small town and all that, he'd already heard of Sue's accident. We were fortunate he'd heard and rushed over because Sue needed more care than the local hospital could provide, what with two broken ribs, a concussion, and a collapsed lung, among other bumps and bruises.

Eugenio told the ambulance driver to take her to the San Augustin Clinic, a private hospital in Loja, widely regarded as the best in the city. We would've had no idea where to go, and there's a definite difference in the quality of medical care in Ecuador depending upon the sign over the door.

San Augustin was family-run by two brothers, both surgeons trained in the States. They spoke English. Sue spent three days there, recovering in a nice private room with a private bath, satellite TV, telephone, and three edible meals a day. The nursing staff knew no English but took great care of her. I'd considered sleeping on the room's sofa, we roughing it in the year since we'd moved before we began renovating our house. Instead, I ended up going home that evening, I of no use in Loja with Sue sedated.

As you may have guessed, Sue recovered. However, on the sharper turns, for a while anyway, I had to help her steer our "new" 1974 Toyota FJ40, as it lacked power steering, and Sue's ribs were sore for months. All in all, it was a good outcome, though, considering what could've happened.

Now imagine what her medical care would've cost in the States - a trip to an emergency room, a 25-mile ambulance ride, treatment from two surgeons, a tube inserted into Sue's side to inflate her lung, medications, that private room with a private bath, satellite TV, telephone, and three edible meals a day, plus a few things I've forgotten. Care to take a guess what the bill was? A to Z…

Was it $744? Obviously, we wish Sue'd not been thrown from the horse, "Bad horse!" but we learned medical care in Ecuador was just fine and cheap enough that pay-as-you-go really was a viable option. Even so, neither of us has saddled up since.

068

STADIUMS IN HIS SANDBOX

My job interview had taken an awkward turn. While impressed with my thesis project, "A New Stadium for Milwaukee," David, my interviewer, was finding it hard to believe a recent graduate with no experience could be so knowledgeable about ballparks. He didn't say it, but I got the feeling he thought one of my thesis committee members, Gabe Paul Jr., then Vice-President of Stadium Operations for the Milwaukee Brewers, had done much of the design work for me.

So I repeated what Gabe, the man in charge of the Brewers' actual project for a new stadium, said to open my thesis defense, "I'm impressed. He's done more by himself in four months than a whole team of architects has done for me in over a year for a million dollars." Sensing David was still not convinced, I pointed to my resume, Gabe's contact info, "Call. Ask."

The interview at the architectural firm HOK Sport (now Populous) in Kansas City was my first after earning a Master of Architecture degree at the University of Wisconsin-Milwaukee. As luck would have it, I got a hard-to-impress interviewer, but as the human resources guy, it was David's job to be skeptical of job seekers like me, so I didn't take it personally.

That and I didn't want to ruin my chances because working at HOK Sport, the world leader in sports facility architecture, had been my dream job ever since I discovered it was possible to design stadiums and arenas for a living. Why I was thrilled to learn HOK would be one of the firms represented at the School of Architecture and Urban Planning's Career Day just weeks before I'd graduate. The fact that HOK's representative was from their St. Louis office, specializing in medical facilities, mattered not.

So eager to speak with anyone at HOK, I arrived for my interview ahead of the person scheduled ahead of me. When it was my turn, I told the interviewer straight away that I had no interest in hospitals. Instead, I showed her what I was working on, my nearly complete thesis project. She had no trouble connecting the dots, setting aside her literature from St. Louis. The pressure off, we filled my time slot with pleasant conversation as she scribbled notes all over my resume, just far enough away that even my then 20/20 eyes couldn't read what she wrote.

At the end of our interview, she assured me she'd contact the Kansas City office on my behalf. A few weeks later, after I'd jumped through my final hoop at UWM, HOK Sport in Kansas City did indeed call, asking if I could make my way down for an interview.

"Absolutely!"

While interested, they were unwilling to foot the bill. For a recent graduate with no experience, sure, but I think maybe one of those notes scribbled in the margins of my resume was that for a chance to interview with HOK Sport, I'd pay my way. And I would, as I wanted them to see my enthusiasm, figuring it would pay off later, even if it left me with little leverage early.

Flooding was a major problem in the Midwest during the spring and summer of 1990. It became a problem for me when yet another massive storm system blew through the Kansas City area, forcing the cancellation of my flight from Milwaukee. All dressed up with no place to go, I called HOK from a pay phone at Mitchell Field, informing them that not only had the airline canceled my flight, but they told me it didn't look good for later in the day.

I barely relayed that information when I heard <KA-BOOM> over the phone. Concurring with the forecast the airline had given me, the woman on the other end asked if the next day would be OK.

"Absolutely!"

The following morning, my flight left as scheduled despite more stormy weather in the Kansas City area. From my window seat at 37,000 feet, I could see the extent of flooding in the Midwest - the Great Plains looking more like the Great Lakes. After circling the airport long enough to raise my anxiety another level or two, I finally made it to Kansas City. Almost, for only after I checked in at the rental car counter did I discover a twenty-mile drive awaited me to reach HOK's downtown office.

Entering the building, I was an uncomfortable mix of nerves and excitement. Then there was Kansas City's summer heat and humidity, my suit and tie, and a new pair of not-yet broken-in dress shoes adding to my discomfort. Even so, I still remembered what Del told me - that when I walked into a business, from the owner to the janitor, treat everyone with respect... because it's the right thing to do. And I'd never know who the hiring person would talk to about me. I was to be particularly pleasant to support staff because they were often gatekeepers - the first people the people doing the hiring would ask, "What did you think of that guy?"

Of course, the first thing HOK's receptionist told me was, "I'm sorry, Mr. Curran, but your interview will be delayed."

Who is this, Mr. Curran? Oh, wait, that's me...

"No problem!"

And it was because what became a two-hour delay allowed me to check out all the photos, drawings, and models of the firm's projects on display in their lobby. As I did, various employees popped in to apologize, telling me, "It'll just be another 15 minutes," the same way a pilot announces on the intercom, "It'll just be another 15 minutes," every 15 minutes, for an hour and a half. Feeling like a kid in a candy store, they could've left me there all day, especially if I'd been wearing comfortable shoes. Or no shoes.

When I finally got my interview with David, then the Personnel Director, now a Senior Architect/ Principal at Populous, he also apologized for the lengthy delay, explaining the reason I was kept waiting was that he and others were on a conference call, HOK awarded the project for a new arena in Anaheim, California the night before. While we were the only two in the open-plan office's centrally located conference room, the surrounding walls were mostly glass, so I strained to focus on the task. I was still that kid in the candy store, looking at everything.

Including the resume I handed the woman from the St. Louis office. When David opened my file, there it was, the margins filled with her handwritten notes. Too far away to read when she wrote them, this time, I got a good enough look, even upside down, to read the one at the top, above my name - "This guy was building stadiums in his sandbox."

I didn't see what else she wrote, but she got that right, as I long had "a thing" for stadiums. The first I ever visited, professional size, came courtesy of Del calling in a favor as a former Sports Director at KMOX to not only get us in but down on the field of (old) Busch Stadium in St. Louis, in the middle of winter, and Ma and Del's honeymoon. Yes, they brought me along and took me on a stadium tour. I know, right? St. Louis? But it didn't seem strange to me because I was nine years old, and what else would newlyweds do on their honeymoon?

A few years later, when the Louisiana Superdome would've still had that new stadium smell, we stayed in New Orleans for a couple-two-three days during one of our annual family driving vacations. Of course, I was eager to see the inside of what was then the world's largest indoor stadium, but we couldn't get in the door. Wouldn't you know it? There was a Church of Christ convention. No entry except for attendees. To this day, I hold a mild grudge against the CoC.

Then there was the time we stopped for the night in Calgary, Alberta, on yet another annual family driving vacation. Our hotel was near the home of the Canadian Football League's Calgary Stampeders, McMahon Stadium. I just had to see a Canadian stadium, so with Ma riding shotgun, Del drove me over as rain began to fall. When Del got "close enough" to the stadium, I hopped out of the back seat, not waiting for him to come to a complete stop. After Del did, he and Ma remained in the car. No interest, I guess.

Unable to get a good look through the fence surrounding the stadium, I did what any aficionado would do - I jumped on top of a dumpster to get a better look over the fence. Standing on garbage in the pouring rain to look inside an empty stadium in

Calgary, I'm sure Ma and Del were left to wonder, "What's wrong with that boy?" Even though my future wife may well have been no more than a few miles away, I'm not sure I would've climbed on top of garbage in the pouring rain to get a look at her... then.

OK, so I never built stadiums in my sandbox, but I would stand on garbage in the pouring rain to see one, and with that woman's note topping my resume, how could my interview not go well? But as it did, it didn't. I think. Maybe. I don't know. I still don't know. I probably never will.

One of the reasons I met with Gabe only twice as I worked on my thesis project was that I didn't want anyone wondering what David apparently was - if my project was more Gabe's than mine. So much for that strategy, but at least I could and did confidently point to Gabe's contact information, knowing he would set the record straight.

David broke the awkwardness of the moment by motioning to a passing colleague to join us. After exchanging pleasantries, David got the impromptu guest up to speed, showing him my thesis project and resume and pointing to the note at the top. Perhaps stalling until he'd had time to examine my work, the mystery guest inquired about my 10-year experience as a sternwheel paddleboat captain, Kansas City having one the firm partied on a time or ten.

While his comment on my project wouldn't match Gabe's to open my thesis defense, I tried not to smile too wide when he said, "We have people working here who couldn't do this." He then asked if the work was mine. I assured him it was, as I again pointed to Gabe's contact info, "Call. Ask." After an affirmative head nod, he then excused himself, continuing on his previous path.

David then told me, "Not to be rude, but I didn't introduce him because I didn't want you to be nervous."

"No problem. I knew who he was. Dennis Wellner. Designed Joe Robbie Stadium in Miami."

"Who… are you?" David didn't say that, but given his reaction, he may as well have because pre-Internet, not only did I know the name of the architect who designed Joe Robbie Stadium, but I recognized him when I saw him. Dennis was also a founder of HOK Sport and is now a Senior Principal at Populous. Last time I checked, he'd overseen the design of 14 National Football League stadiums. Really. If you don't believe me, "Call. Ask."

The interview seemed to go better after that as David and I discussed salary, benefits, and all the other stuff I should but don't find all that interesting. David said he couldn't give me a hiring decision, as they'd have to assess their staffing needs after getting the Anaheim arena project. He went on to explain that HOK Sport never wanted to lay off anyone because of the highly specialized nature of their business, preferring to work shorthanded rather than hire people on a temporary basis, so he'd figure out where they were and then contact me.

I thanked David for his time and asked him to thank Dennis, expressing how much I appreciated the opportunity. Before exiting the building, I thanked the receptionist, telling her how much I enjoyed my time in their lobby. As I walked out the door, smiling from ear to ear, my dream job all but bagged, I thought to myself, "These shoes aren't so bad."

With a sunrise flight to Milwaukee, I drove to the Harry S Truman Sports Complex for a Kansas City Royals baseball game. Arriving well before most fans, I took the opportunity to change into comfortable clothes. The weather had cleared, the night perfect for baseball in one of the finest stadium complexes ever built, even if it was in the middle of an asphalt lot.

I didn't think the evening could get any better. Still, it did, because on sale at the stadium's concession stands was my favorite bratwurst, Johnsonville, at the time, not for sale at Milwaukee's County Stadium. After the game, I returned to the Kansas City airport. To save money I didn't have, I passed on a night at a hotel and instead slept in the car, parked outside the locked gate of the rental return lot.

Back in Wisconsin, I sent HOK a thank you letter, telling them how much I enjoyed my extended afternoon in their office. A few days later, I received a note from David reiterating what he'd said at the end of my interview - that they'd get back to me when they had a grasp on their staffing needs.

Days passed... Then weeks... Then months... I never heard from HOK again. Not even a rejection letter, even after I sent them another letter more or less asking for one. My Uncle David, who had far more experience dealing with architects as facility manager for Caterpillar in Minneapolis, said HOK probably didn't hire me because I knew too much for an entry-level position. They didn't send me a rejection letter because they didn't want me to go away mad, just go away, gain some experience, and then come back, so management need not explain to staff why a recent graduate was above them in the pecking order.

While that made sense, I remembered something Del once said, "A good company will always find a place for a good person." So, was I not a good person? Or were they not a good company? To be fair, I figured that despite the comment written at the top of my resume by the woman from the St. Louis office, HOK

Sport just didn't know what to do with the guy who showed up to the interview in Kansas City.

So, for reasons unknown, I didn't get my dream job, the one for which I was never more qualified. Despite my profound disappointment, my interest in sports facility architecture never waned. I've continued to work on my thesis project while following the development and construction of new stadiums and arenas worldwide. There have been many, the years since my interview with HOK a "Golden Age" in sports facility architecture. A Golden Age I missed.

One of my favorite quotes is from one of my favorite movies, *Patton*. After being relieved of his duties during World War II, the title character proclaimed with unrestrained frustration, "The last great opportunity of a lifetime... an entire world at war, and I'm left out of it? God will not permit this to happen! I will be allowed to fulfill my destiny!"

General George S. Patton eventually fulfilled his destiny, the one he envisioned. I'm still working on mine, just not the one I'd envisioned. I'll never know what would've been had HOK Sport in Kansas City hired me in 1990. What I do know is that if they had, many of the stories in my books would be about different people, places, and things...

I should send HOK another thank you letter.

069

MY STUPID HUMAN TRICK

The first time I called my first real boss "Mr. Meighan," I was told, "Pat, just call me Pat," so for the next ten years, it was "Pat," and "Mimi," his co-owner wife. I liked that everyone at Clear Water Harbor was on a first-name basis, the lack of formality befitting what was a family business, one that grew exponentially in my ten years there. I don't know if calling the owners by their first name played a part in the Harbor's success, but I do know calling Pat and Mimi "Pat" and "Mimi" didn't lead to a civilization breakdown.

Wanting to transport that workplace spirit with me, I would never again refer to any boss as "Dr.," "Mr.," "Mrs.," or "Ms." (there never was a "Miss"). Even though my next (and final) four jobs were all the necktie variety, I referred to my bosses - Tom, George, Graham, Farid, Howard, and Jackie - by their first names. Even though I worked with several colleagues who insisted on formality when it came to addressing superiors, no one ever called me on calling them by their first name.

There was one colleague - there's always one - who insisted we call him "Dr. Timothy," so "Tim" it was, for me anyway. He may have earned his title, but never my respect, as all his students would've failed after his first semester teaching at United Arab Emirates University had the boss not changed their grades to avoid embarrassing our unit. Realizing he had no business in the classroom, management promoted him to management, where I still called him "Tim" until management fired him.

Some probably said, although not to my face, that referring to the man or woman in charge by their first name was impolite, even disrespectful, but other than when I called Tim "Tim," it never was. Given that I was on a first-name basis with management for nearly 30 years, and it didn't lead to a civilization breakdown, my lack of... manners... didn't matter, helped by the fact most of my bosses were for jobs in the UAE, where everyone was on a culturally correct first name basis.

Sometimes, though, knowing and showing proper etiquette does matter, particularly in another, far different culture. Just ask the more than a few Westerners who flew into the UAE with every intention of getting a business deal done but returned home without it even being discussed. Why? Because Emiratis valued personal relationships, many unwilling to do business until they sized up a potential partner, often multiple meetings necessary before negotiations began. For Westerners, who generally want everything done yesterday, having to build a personal relationship before a professional one could be a number of adjectives, none of them positive, many preceded and/or followed by curse words.

Once I understood Emiratis' need to know with whom they were dealing, teaching my students got a whole lot easier. Their attitude on Day 1 of class was often, "I am your student, let's see if you are my teacher," they far more interested in learning about me than the course material. Why I spent the first few days ignoring the syllabus to talk with my students, allowing them to get to know me. Eager to aid the process, I told them they could ask any question, I promising I'd answer, just maybe not the way they hoped I would.

On Day 1, I also told each class I'd never lie to them, then asked why I made such a promise. In each class, at least one student knew, "Sir, because if we catch you lying, we will never believe anything you say." And I needed my students to believe me, to trust me, so they'd try and succeed after I told them they could do something they didn't think they could. This was particularly true when I taught first-year computer programming students, many doubting they could learn to tell a computer what to do in its language.

"Sir, English is difficult. Now you want me to learn Computer?"

On the first day of class, before anything else, introductions were in order. As a blue-eyed, pale-skinned American man walking into a classroom of Emirati women dressed in black, the tension was palpable as I did not know them, and they did not know me. A tense classroom was not something I wanted, so the first thing I did after saying "Hello" was to let my students know the answer to the question they were all asking themselves, "What's the teacher going to be like this semester?" by writing my name on the whiteboard… in Arabic.

جان روبرت كران

The act was simple, but one that made an immediate connection with my new students because I used their language, one far different from my own, one they surely never expected I would, or even could.

Moreover, I wrote my name in Arabic (right-to-left, of course) with confidence, as if I'd been doing it all my life. Written in their language, they had an easier time pronouncing my name, with a little help from me, since it didn't translate perfectly into Arabic. Why, over the years, I saw John pronounced as Jan, Joan, Jane, and my favorite, Goon. "I am Mister Goon."

Having learned to pronounce my name, my students pleaded for me to write it in English... imagine that. So I did, under the Arabic version, writing my name in English, right-to-left, flipped horizontally, my name appearing as it would if viewed from behind the whiteboard.

ИАЯЯUƆ TЯƎⱭOЯ ИHOႱ

Not only did I have their attention, but I had them laughing... and wondering how I could write backward as quickly as most could forward.

That was not my final trick, though, because once I sensed that version was losing steam, I gave my students another to think about by writing my name right-to-left and upside down, flipped horizontally and vertically, my name appearing as it would if my students stood on their heads.

ИVЯЯUƆ TЯƎⱭOЯ NHOႱ

Amazed at how I could write backward and upside down so quickly, I not only had their attention, but I had them laughing as they contorted their bodies, trying to make my writing "right." Writing my name in Arabic not only demonstrated to my students that I cared enough to learn what even they told me was a difficult language, but my stupid human trick also let them know what kind of teacher I would be, what kind of class I wanted, and what I expected of my students.

Talking with my students those first few days put us behind schedule, but I viewed that time as an investment, one that always paid off when we got down to business. Because my students trusted me, they followed me wherever I took them without hesitation, so we made up for "lost" time in no time.

The inspiration for my take on teachers writing their names on the board the first day of class was a "How To Draw" lesson that asked the potential Picasso to draw, from memory, a familiar but common object, like a chair... upside down. Try it sometime. While more difficult than it sounds, the exercise is a good warm-up before writing backward and then backward and upside down, my stupid human trick.

070

GET LOST, KID

The car was stuck in the mud, and despite Del's best efforts, getting unstuck would require help - more than an 11-year-old boy and his mother could muster. We tried everything, even putting the car's floor mats under the rear tires, but as soon as Del pressed the accelerator, they turned into flying carpets.

A "PORCUPINE!" had ambled across the road in front of us as Del drove Ma's 1973 Dodge Charger with its 400 cubic-inch engine, wasted on a not-built-for-speed dirt road in the Chequamegon-Nicolet National Forest in northeast Wisconsin. Riding shotgun, Ma was excited to see what she'd never seen. I'd never seen a "quill pig" either, but sitting in the back, by the time I got a look over the high-backed bucket seats, it was already across the road, down and up the ditch.

Once into the woods, the porcupine's pace slowed enough that Del parked the car on the side of the lane-and-a-half-wide road so we could get out for a better look. At a porcupine that didn't seem at all concerned with us. Perhaps it had never seen humans before. Or maybe it had, why it raised its "round little rump to us," as Del told his listeners the following Monday morning during his call-in show, *Dial Del*.

It wasn't long before we couldn't see the porcupine because the trees were too thick. So we walked back to the car to find that in the short time spent watching the porcupine moon us, the ditch-side wheels of the Charger had sunk almost to the axle in the road's shoulder, softened by the spring thaw and rain.

We weren't out for a joy ride that morning in May. We were in the woods with a purpose. Well, Ma was, for deeper into the forest was a group of Waupaca High School students who'd spent the week camping, part of a school program my friend Roger had participated in the year before. He told me his week stirred a lifelong love of camping and canoeing, as evidenced by his yearly trips to the woods and lakes of Canada in Ontario's Quetico Provincial Park.

Ma wasn't in the Chequamegon-Nicolet National Forest to camp or canoe - her idea of roughing it staying at a Holiday Inn, with no swimming pool, even though she never learned to swim. No, Ma was there to deliver an English lesson to the students, no doubt her delayed teaching session causing them unimaginable distress.

With no traffic and no one else with reason to drive in the forest on a dreary day, we agreed that waiting for help was pointless. So we walked down the road, intent on reaching the campsite where there'd be plenty of help to get us unstuck. There weren't many road options in the woods, but we encountered a T less than a mile from the porcupine sighting.

With a decision to make - left or straight - Ma and Del pulled out the map. Their standing side-by-side forced me to look at the map upside-down. Even so, what I saw told me left was the way to go, but Ma and Del agreed we should go straight. Outnumbered in everything that mattered except map-reading ability, I followed, knowing we were going the wrong way.

After another mile or so, we reached another T in the road, which offered the option of turning either left or right. It was here that Ma and Del realized their mistake reading the map at the previous T, so backtrack we did... in silence... although inside my head was a voice that sounded a lot like mine screaming, "I TOLD YOU WE SHOULD GO LEFT!"

Figuring the walk past the car and out of the forest shorter than to the campsite, we again walked straight instead of taking the right where we should've gone left. Just outside the entry to the forest, we were fortunate to find a farmer, with a tractor, an old one, an Allis-Chalmers, what little paint remaining, orange. After explaining our plight, the farmer was willing to sacrifice his time to pull the Charger from the mud, which he did. After Del slipped the man a few bucks for his trouble, we piled into the car and headed for the campsite, taking the left at the T we should've taken on foot.

Reaching the campsite hours late, Ma canceled her English lesson on Henry David Thoreau. This is where the term "happy campers" originated... maybe. Instead of her giving a lesson, we sat around the campsite telling the tale of how we came to be stuck in the mud while watching a porcupine flash its backside and then walking for miles before being rescued by a friendly farmer.

After enough of that, the students offered to take me for a walk in the woods where they'd spent the past week. Despite the miles I'd already logged, I was eager to go on a walkabout with the big kids, Ma and Del no doubt just as eager to get some time away from the boy who told them to go left.

Deeper into the woods we walked, I delighting in the opportunity to look at this and that. And in such a forest, there's plenty of this and that, as well as "What's this?" and "What's that?" why I feel more at home in the woods than almost any other place. At the time, I didn't know about this Thoreau guy, but if Ma had presented her lesson, his story would've gotten my attention.

What did get my attention, even though I was trailing the group, looking at e v e r y t h i n g, was that their forward progress had halted…

"Anyone know the way back?"

"No."

"Anyone bring a compass?"

"Left mine at camp."

"Dumbass."

"What are we going to do?"

'I don't know."

They then broke their huddle, the leader telling me, "John, don't be scared, but we're lost."

Lost, or just pretending to be? I was eleven. What did I know? For one, where I was. "Follow me."

Follow they did. On the walk out, even though I gave Nature a thorough going over, I always kept track of where I was. Why, a half an hour or so later, after a walk back about as straight as possible through a dense forest, the campsite came into view through the filter of trees.

"John, please, please, please don't tell your mother we got you lost."

"…but you didn't get me lost."

When we reached the campsite, Ma asked the students, "How was your walk in the woods?"

"Sorry. We tried, but we couldn't lose your son."

I was never sure whether they were lost or just pretending to be hoping to scare their teacher's son, but either way, I never ratted them out… until now.

186

071

WORKING ON CHRISTMAS

Nasser stuck his head in my classroom door to ensure I was present only one day each year, December 25. Knowing that management at United Arab Emirates University tasked him with going around to the classrooms of presumed Christian faculty to ensure they were at work, I never gave him any grief over it. Nasser, a Palestinian and a Muslim, was a good guy stuck with a lousy job.

"Mister John is here!" I'd say, as Nasser would smile to hide his embarrassment before backing his head out the door. Nasser knew I never missed a day of work, but he still had to check - trust, but verify. In the days leading up to the holiday, I warned new faculty they'd better be at work too or face the possibility of being terminated. In the UAE, losing your job meant losing your residence visa and your residence, not that you'd need either after being deported.

"Merry Christmas!"

All but a couple-two-three of the fourteen times the holiday came and went while I lived in the United Arab Emirates, I had to work on Christmas, December 25 just another day on the calendar in the predominantly Muslim country. As it is for many others, even in predominantly Christian countries, working on Christmas was just a part of the job. I only got the holiday off when Christmas fell on a weekend or an Emirati holiday.

Known to dress for work with a certain.... panache, I took the opportunity to color coordinate on Christmas by wearing a white dress shirt along with a bright red tie that matched my pants... and something I otherwise never wore to work - a hat, a Santa hat, for reasons unknown, one I packed in my 17 boxes of belongings air freighted to Abu Dhabi after I moved to the UAE in July 1991.

The students loved the droopily conical red hat trimmed in faux white fur, resembling The Grinch's homemade hat assembled at his home on Mount Crumpet. The only frowns ever shot my way came from a few Muslim faculty members and then only those in the Arabic Department, perhaps more conservative than those who worked with me in the Math and Computer Department, who never made a face or a fuss.

While UAEU management wanted to be sure I was at work on Christmas, they didn't care if I wore a Santa hat. Such was not the case when I worked at Dubai Women's College as the director there threatened to terminate anyone making such an overt display of the holiday. If you were wondering, he was an American, a Christian... and a few other adjectives.

Even though I couldn't wear my Santa hat, I still looked forward to spending Christmas at work, with my Muslim students. I can't say the same for some of my Christian colleagues who whined about having to work on the holiday, especially if they were married with children.

"You signed up for this, remember? 'Member?'"

For me, celebrating the day with my students - my family away from family - was Christmas. Even "The Grinch" director couldn't stop them from wishing me a "Merry Christmas," or giving me a card, the occasional gift, and chocolates or other assorted goodies, any excuse to party and get out of learning something, in the curriculum anyway. In return, I shared my homemade Christmas cookies with them and any colleagues I didn't want to push down a stairwell.

"Merry Christmas!"

Covered in various colors of neon-bright frosting, with sprinkles and such, the ladies delighted in the variety of cookies - snowmen, Christmas trees, reindeer, angels, candy canes, Santas, stars, bells, mittens, etc. Explaining the significance of each shape added "flavor" to the cutout cookies I learned to make as a kid, "helping" Grandma Curran with her seasonal production. Many of the tin molds I used to cut out those cookies were Grandma's, which she gave me after she retired from the kitchen.

All mouths with my cookies, the students were all ears as I told them stories of baking with Grandma when I was barely tall enough to see over her kitchen counters. Much as they enjoyed the stories, I'm sure they thought my homemade cookies an even better treat. So good, they had a culturally difficult time believing a mere man could've created such deliciousness...

"Mister John... you made these?"

"Yes."

"Sure?"

"Yes."

"Mister John, one day you make some woman very happy."

Sue?

072

SCRAMBLED EGGS

The only time I've performed the honor, I was anxious, suffering far more than I do now from torn rotator cuffs in each shoulder, the left, especially bad. So, of course, I ended up on the right side of the casket, my left arm left to do most of the work a pallbearer does, on behalf of my Great Uncle Ed.

Much as I like to make memories, I didn't want my wonky shoulder to. With the help of five others, it didn't, Ed's casket arriving safely at the hearse parked in front of the dozen or so steps fronting St. Paul's Catholic Church in Bloomer, Wisconsin. Go on, admit it… you're a little disappointed, aren't you?

I didn't know Ed that well, as he and his brother George were reserved, which was unusual for Ma's side of the family. They said so little that most of what I recall about them I learned not from them but from others - the childhood accident that cost Ed an eye, his brother George shooting an arrow into the sky… and that neither ever married.

I always wondered whether the first had anything to do with the second - Ed feeling shy, George feeling guilty - because others told me George was once a ladies' man. The one thing I can tell you about Ed, again because others told me, was that he was tight with his money. Why I was surprised but pleased that to help with the out-of-state tuition I'd be paying as a University of Florida freshman, Ed sent me a check for $1500... after vetting me.

I got that - after watching Ma and Del each blow a gasket when they discovered Jay had blown a $1000 gift from his mother on a top-of-the-line stereo system. Jay was a deejay at WOKL 1050 Radio, but Ma and Del were none too happy that money didn't go for his tuition at UW-Eau Claire. Just a spectator to the conflict, it wasn't the first time I benefitted from having someone seven years older around, someone discovering the boundaries I then avoided.

Born on July 4, 1899, Ed lived long enough to see a return on his investment when I graduated from UW-Milwaukee in 1987 with not one but two degrees. He didn't quite make it to my third, breathing his last on February 3, 1990, just a couple of weeks after I began work on my thesis project, just a couple of weeks after Professor Keegan informed me his cancer had returned.

Given what Ed had done for me, I was "happy" I could attend his funeral, honored to serve as a pallbearer, my schedule flexible for the first time in years, I living in Waupaca with Ma. Even though I never worked more than I did that last semester, rarely getting more than two hours of sleep each night, I couldn't remain in the dorms, open only to full-time students, because, according to UWM, with my thesis counting but six credits, I was a part-timer.

With my shoulder holding, the only other thing I remember about Ed's funeral happened after the service, at the reception in the church basement. Sitting across a folding table from my Uncle Dennis - also seven years older than me, the youngest of Ma's five sisters and two brothers - talk turned to my just-under-way thesis project, "A New Stadium for Milwaukee," and my plan of working at HOK Sport in Kansas City after I graduated. Having just about exhausted the topic, Dennis told me, "I really admire you for putting all your eggs in one basket."

Then, my plan didn't go as planned. HOK refused to play along by hiring me, never getting back to me after my interview, even after I sent them a letter more or less asking for closure. Left with no choice but to move on, my dream job once so close, now out of reach, the first thing I did was apply for a job at HOK Sport's competitor, also in Kansas City, Ellerbe Beckett. They sent me a form rejection letter.

Fresh out of firms specializing in sports facility design, I had to apply for "any" architecture job. The poor economy made matters worse, with few architecture jobs for which to apply. One "business" that was hiring architects was the CIA. When I told Ma I'd applied, she sighed, "Great, one more son who can't tell me what he does for a living," Jay already working in intelligence for the U.S. Army, or so he said. With top-level security clearance, he couldn't say much about what he did without risking a stay in Leavenworth. After applying, I never heard from the CIA either... or did I?

Another of the few openings I found was for an entry-level position at an architecture firm in Grand Forks, North Dakota. While North Dakota is a beautiful state, it's not because of its architecture, but with nothing else going for me, I called. The hiring man wanted me to come up for an interview, but like HOK, his firm wouldn't pay my way. His firm not HOK, and I then that much poorer, I told him I couldn't afford to, so a telephone interview it was.

That he was still willing to hire me, sight unseen, indicated his desperation. North Dakota, apparently, was not a draw for architects. Then he told me the starting salary. North Dakota wasn't the problem as he offered me not much more than I made piloting the Chief Waupaca. So I told him, as politely as I could, "Thanks, but no thanks, I didn't go to university for nine years to get paid that...," and what I didn't say, "... for a job with no horn to toot or bell to ring, working on projects I have little interest in."

Not liking to do what I don't like to do, I was lukewarm about another opportunity at a small-town architecture firm, even though this one was in my old hometown of Eau Claire. Scheduled for a Saturday morning, I arrived early for my interview. My interviewer, even earlier, his Audi the only car in the parking lot. Qualifying as one of those job interview nightmares, I couldn't get inside the building... the doors locked.

I knocked, pounded, and yelled, but there was no response. Walking around the building, peering in the windows, I saw no one, so I drove off, calling my interviewer from a pay phone at the Holiday Inn just up the street. When I returned, he stood at the door, claiming it was unlocked. I know it wasn't - I know how to open doors, three-time college graduate and all - he just didn't want to admit it. Guess how that interview went?

Difficult as it was getting in the door, I couldn't wait to get out. At least HOK was impressed with my work. Enough, my interviewer called in the firm's founder to have a look, but this guy barely said a word. Like HOK, though, he never got back to me. Just as well, as my Uncle Mike didn't have anything good to say about the firm or its owner. However, my Grandma

Curran, with visions of me working close to her home, was disappointed. I wasn't. Neither was Mike.

To be fair, I had little to show a potential employer other than my two design projects with Kent, "The Platonic Pavilion" and my thesis project, both irrelevant to most firms, especially those in Grand Forks and Eau Claire. The only other project I was proud to show was my working model of an air-supported domed stadium. However, watching it inflate in person was way cooler than it appeared in my portfolio, in a series of time-lapse photographs, and it too may have lacked relevance.

Not finding any architecture jobs, I broadened my search, applying for a city manager position in a small Wisconsin town. Much to my surprise, I made it through the first two rounds, coming up one round short of being a finalist. The city council cited my lack of experience, apparently not counting my time as the Mayor of Funkytown on the new computer game *Sim City*. Their loss because if my *Sim City* experience carried over, that town's population would've grown to millions, the city's treasury overflowing with Simoleons.

Then along came the opening that opened my eyes - teaching CAD and architectural design to students at a technical school in Thief River Falls, Minnesota, who would then move on to a four-year program. Apparently, no one wanted to teach in Thief River Falls, conveniently located to Grand Forks, North Dakota - 44 miles distant - and nowhere else, as I would've been hired on the spot simply because no one else wanted the job. Why the Minnesota nice woman-in-charge, Mary, did her darndest to get me hired. Much to her disappointment, no matter what approach she took, I always came up one qualification short... for which she apologized.

Even though I was the only applicant in the race and still lost, it felt good to be wanted. So, as Mary and I said our final goodbyes, I expressed my appreciation for her efforts. I think she was even more disappointed than I was that my teaching career would not begin in Thief River Falls, Minnesota. Every now and then, I imagine how different my life would be if it had.

Still, I was disappointed, more than I thought I'd be, so when I came across another opportunity to teach, I pursued it. Not only because teaching had piqued my interest, but so too did doing it in another country, in another culture. In the end, I just wasn't interested, not so much in Japan, but in the subject, English, so I declined the offer.

Good thing I did, given my four-week experience substitute teaching an English class my first year at United Arab Emirates University. Afterward, I told my supervisor, "Don't ever ask me to teach English again. It's not fair to the students." Even though I tested out of English at three universities without ever taking an English class, I had no idea how to teach it, not remembering how I learned it.

Scanning classified newspaper ads, lacking in listings for architecture jobs, I wondered why I'd not instead studied accounting, nursing, or welding, as there were always numerous ads for those professions… taunting me. Then I'd taunt myself, "Why didn't HOK hire me? This would've been so easy! I'd be getting paid to do what I love!"

I trudged on, pursuing another teaching job that would've put my other degree to use - teaching economics at Fox Valley Tech in nearby Appleton. The woman I talked to couldn't tell me not to apply but that I shouldn't bother without a Ph.D., as they already had over 40 candidates with terminal degrees. I guess architecture graduates weren't the only ones wishing they'd taken up accounting, nursing, or welding.

Despite finishing my formal education, I was still learning lessons, like how hard it was to find a job without one, especially in a tough economy. Bad as it was, my situation worsened six months after graduation as I had to start paying back my student loans - over $50,000 at 9 and 10% interest, adjusted for inflation, over $100,000 in 2020 dollars. For the next ten years, I would owe the bank nearly $400 a month, and they would own me. Why I made a vow that once my debt was paid (and I paid it back early), never again would I owe anyone money - a vow I have kept.

Come New Year's Day, I started counting the days until mid-March when Pat and Mimi would return from Key Largo, Florida, and I'd be back working at Clear Water Harbor. Some days, with no job and little hope of finding one, I'd take the ten-minute walk to Clear Water Harbor to see the Chief Waupaca, the boat my happy place, where I always felt I belonged. Covered in snow and frozen in its dock on Taylor Lake, my old friend looked as forlorn as I surely did, the months after my interview with HOK soul-crushing. Little did I know, my situation was about to get even more worser.

THE END... OF THIS BOOK

THANK YOU!

Next in the series, **MISFIT 3**, has 36 more stories.

ENJOY!

MISTERJOHN.ME

yakpublishing.com

Milton Keynes UK
Ingram Content Group UK Ltd.
UKHW041303290924
1905UKWH00001B/1